The 716
Love &
Consequences

Copyright © 2017 A.A. Lewis

All rights reserved. No part of this book may be reproduced in any form or by any electronic or mechanical means, including information storage and retrieval systems, without permission in writing from the publisher, except by reviewers, who may quote brief passages in a review.

The characters and events contained in this book are fictitious. Any similarities to real persons, living or dead and or events are coincidental and not intended by the author.

Credits for use of song titles belong exclusively to the artist named and or the producers and or writers of said songs and or album creators.
Credits for cover design and images by Sheergenius

Printed in the United States of America

Published by D & S Publishing
5047 W, Main St, Kalamazoo, MI 49009
(475) 549-0093
sales@dspublishing.net

****

Acknowledgements

I often ask myself, where would I be if I never attended the Buffalo Academy for the Visual and Performing Arts School for the gifted? Or what if Mr. D'Arcangelo never believed in me? If Mr. Link never pushed me beyond my comfort zone or if Ms. C. Marshall never encouraged me to be great. And I can't forget about Dr. Martin and Mr. Fortunato Pezzimenti among countless other teachers that help mold my impressionable mind to appreciate my gift to create, imagine, be free and willing to express that energy. For that experience I will be forever grateful. And never again will I suppress my creativeness for the black and white of this world. Thank you BAVPA for some of the best years of my life!!

To Nekeisha Baugh-Thompson, Natasha Johnson, Lanita Shaw Daniels, and CeCe Parker.

Thank you for not laughing at me when I told you I had stories and characters in my head trying to break free. Thank you for being a support system for me after all these years. Thank you for being the Friends I've always known. Thank you for taking the time to read, read and read my crazy ideas until I got it right. Your consistent feedback is just what I needed. I appreciate you taking this journey with me.

For my twins, Amina Mabry and Ashanti Banks- Andrew. Thank you for being just as excited in my book as I am. Thank you for encouraging me, reading chapter after chapter and making sure that I captured the vibe of Buffalo with every detail. Thank you for laughing with we, crying with me and helping me remember that life doesn't have to be so serious all the time. I love you ladies! You're the best twins any girl could have in their corner.

To my Sons, thank you for keeping me young. Thank you for loving me unconditionally. You both make my heart rejoice. It doesn't matter what happens in this life, I will always have your back. You both have taught me so many things about myself. Your courage has given me the ability to dream again. I'm so proud to be your mother and I hope that seeing me take a leap of faith can inspire you to follow your dreams no matter what obstacles present themselves throughout your lives. I love you both more than anything in this world. And if you read this book, remember your mother is still and angel!

Thank you, Rosemary, Letricia, Evette, my family and friends that supported my efforts. You mean more to me than you know. I'm surrounded by women with such power, grace, courage and integrity. Thank you for being the circle of support and a foundation for sisters to unite and empower each other. That connection is everything to me and because of your greatness, my cypher is stronger with you in it.

To my dear girlfriends, A. Smith, T. Brown, N. Thompson, L. Daniels, T. Carr, and C. Parker. We may not see each other everyday, or have an opportunity to speak with one another as often as we would like, but when we do it's just like old times. Thank you for making the the 1990's such a great time to be young. I will always cherish our friendships and the life lessons we shared. Love y'all eternally!

Last but not least, to my husband Darryl thank you for loving me, for believing in my dream and pushing me to finish. You are just as creative as I am. Without your essence of hip hop and your knowledge of street life I would have missed capturing the true vibe of the 1990's from a lyrical point of view. I know that this process may have taken me away from you at times, but the patience that you showed and the understanding you displayed proved just how loving and attentive you are. 20 years and counting and the only thing I can think about is how your walk still commands attention, giving me goosebumps and butterflies everytime you walk in a room. Your love is the breeze in spring that brings the bees to the flowers and creates the honey that makes me so sweet. You're my original and for that I'll always be that "Around The Way Girl" in my heart. Loving you till the end… even though you graduated from Burgard!

TABLE OF CONTENTS

ACKNOWLEDGEMENTS	3
CHAPTER ONE	9
CHAPTER TWO	19
CHAPTER THREE	27
CHAPTER FOUR	37
CHAPTER FIVE	43
CHAPTER SIX	49
CHAPTER SEVEN	53
CHAPTER EIGHT	57
CHAPTER NINE	65
CHAPTER TEN	73
CHAPTER ELEVEN	77
CHAPTER TWELVE	81
CHAPTER THIRTEEN	87
CHAPTER FOURTEEN	93

CHAPTER FIFTEEN	109
CHAPTER SIXTEEN	119
CHAPTER SEVENTEEN	125
CHAPTER EIGHTEEN	129
CHAPTER NINETEEN	133
CHAPTER TWENTY	137
CHAPTER TWENTY-ONE	143
CHAPTER TWENTY-TWO	149
CHAPTER TWENTY-THREE	153
CHAPTER TWENTY-FOUR	159
CHAPTER TWENTY-FIVE	163
CHAPTER TWENTY-SIX	165
CHAPTER TWENTY-SEVEN	169
CHAPTER TWENTY-EIGHT	173
CHAPTER TWENTY-NINE	177
CHAPTER THIRTY	181

CHAPTER THIRTY-ONE	185
CHAPTER THIRTY-TWO	191
CHAPTER THIRTY-THREE	197
CHAPTER THIRTY-FOUR	203
CHAPTER THIRTY-FIVE	213
CHAPTER THIRTY-SIX	219
CHAPTER THIRTY-SEVEN	223
CHAPTER THIRTY-EIGHT	229
CHAPTER THIRTY-NINE	233
CHAPTER FORTY	237
CHAPTER FORTY-ONE	243
CHAPTER FORTY-TWO	249
CHAPTER FORTY-THREE	253
CHAPTER FORTY-FOUR	257
CHAPTER FORTY-FIVE	265
CHAPTER FORTY-SIX	269

CHAPTER FORTY-SEVEN	273
CHAPTER FORTY-EIGHT	279
CHAPTER FORTY-NINE	281
CHAPTER FIFTY	287

Chapter One

"So You Like What You See"
— Samuel

"So you like what you see" - Samuell

Anika

It was finally Friday, I felt like the weekend would never get here. It was the week from hell. Not only was it final exam week at on campus but I was finally free of that asshole Quan. I can't believe I spent the last 2 years with that no good bean pie pushin jerk. He'll regret ever losing this. They all do. Now I'm not one to brag, but somewhere between 8th grade and freshman year of high school my body took a change for the better. All that roundness my granny used to call baby fat somehow began to thin out and become defined hips and curves. Not only did I have a small waist, but my perfectly proportioned 36DD's, were a nice addition to my apple shaped ass. I went from a chubby kid to a grown ass woman overnight. At first, I was mortified, how could this be happening to me? But then came the attention. Now don't get me wrong, I loved the way boys and grown ass men looked at me. I could swing my hips and ask a guy to do something for me and they would trip at the chance. But I knew better. My daddy told me with all that power, came a whole lot of problems. My daddy would tell me that girls like me needed to be smarter than other girls. Not only was I pretty, with a nice body, but I was black. "People don't think much of our women" he would say, "Especially black men". My daddy often dropped knowledge on me about the ways of men. He taught me about the hustle men use to run game on women. How not to get caught up in their bull shit and how to switch the game up in my favor. My conversations with my dad were raw and real. He did not hold anything back. And for that I would always be grateful. It made me wise to the game and smarter than most girls out in these streets. But enough about that shit, I need to get up with my girls. It's the "weekennnd babyyy!" as Hookar and Dawn of Buffalo's 93.7 WBLK would say. And nothing gave me more life than releasing some stress on the dance floor and getting my flirt on. And with the week I've had I'm finna act a fool.

"Honk. honk!!" I could hear the bass from the car jumping through the windows of my mother's house. There wasn't a nigga alive that would disrespect me like that. Every dude from CP to Bailey, Doat to Delevan and The Belt to Humboldt knew I was not that type of girl. One, I have 5 brothers all older. Second if you ever thought you had a chance to get with this, you better come with your A Game. I am too damn fine to be jumping at every horn that went beep beep. And last, my mother was not having that loud ass music bangin in front of her house. So all my dudes knew as soon as they hit the middle of E. Ferry Street, they needed to turn that shit down. All that ghettoness could only be one person my girl Monica. "Honk, honk!" I heard a second time, followed by the opening and slamming of the screen door.

"Hey momma Dee!" yelled Monica.

"Hi Monica" my mother said shaking her head. "Where are you two running off too?" she asked.

"To the mall and then to cause some trouble later on tonight!" Monica replied in her usual joking manner.

My mother just shook her head and smiled. By this time Monica had made it back to my room. "Girl why you out there blowing your horn like you somebody's nigga?" I questioned.

"Because, you will never guess who is outside waiting for you?" Monica said with all the excitement of a 3 year old.

She was fixing her hair in my mirror.

"Well who bitch" I demanded.

Monica began to explain as she often did how she met this guy who has a friend and they want to hook up with us. As she began reminiscing about her latest conquest, I slowly zoned out. I was still in my feelings about Quan, I wasn't about to admit it to anyone, but that nigga had me all open. I played the hard to get role, tough girl act, but truth be told I loved him. I really was not feeling like having so dude all in my face right now. The plan was go to the mall get, our outfits for the week-end, and get ready for tonight. I zoned right back into Monica's conversation just in time to hear her say … of the Buffalo Bills.

"Say that again", I asked.

"Oh, so now yo ass paying attention" Monica replied as she nudged me as she was rummaging through my closet. "You heard me bitch, now put this on," she threw a mini skirt from my closet onto the bed with the matching crop top.

"They wanna take us to the mall and hang out, you know that could only mean one thing" Monica paused - "WE ABOUT TO SPEND THAT CASH"- we screamed out loud laughing.

Monica and I finally stepped out onto the porch only to be greeted by 2 of my older brothers, about 7 of their friends and a host of screaming female groupies all admiring the all black Benz with tinted windows and the customized rims that was parked in front of my house. To top it off, the number 13 Utica bus pulled over once the driver and a few the passengers noticed who was leaning against the car. Many people got off the bus to get a better look or a chance at an autograph. We stood there in amazement at how these people were acting.

They were acting as though they had never met a famous person before. Our suitors were busy signing autographs and taking pictures with their fans. Once the ball players noticed that we were waiting they cleared through the crowd and made their way up to the porch. Monica made introductions as if I did not know who he was. I could feel the eyes of people checking me out. I even heard a female say, "Isn't that Quan's girl"? another girl whispered, "doesn't she date that rapper dude"? I have no time or energy to give to haters. The only eyes I was concerned about was my date's. From the look on his face he was pleasantly surprised. He took my hand and guided me to the car, opened the door and helped me into the back seat of the car. Monica sat in the front seat of the car with her friend. They were engaged in conversation that I could barely hear due to the heavy bass and loud lyrics of LL's "Cars ride by with the boomin systems" echoing through the car. I sat in the back seat looking out the window. Mr. Cornerback touched my hand and leaned in closer to me. He whispered how beautiful I was and that Monica did not do me justice. I blushed as I turned to look at him. He sat there looking at me as though I was the last thing he was ever going to eat. His dark complexion, chiseled body, and pristine white smile would make any girl wet with temptation. I could tell that he was fresh from the barber shop. He sported a well defined crisp edge up. He smelled all of Fahrenheit and was wearing a pair of Karl Kani black jeans with a v-neck black rayon tee with the signature Karl Kani logo on the front of the tee. Around his neck was a single gold rope chain with a cross attached. He topped it off with a pair of black Timb's. He was not as flashy as other ballers I've seen or met. He did not have a grille or gold teeth - thank god. From first glance you would have thought he was just another average guy.

We arrived at the Galleria Mall. He opened my door like a perfect gentleman.

Took my hand and lead the way into the mall through the double doors of Kaufmann's department store. As we walked through the doors he asked, "if I was the jealous type".

I replied "No".

He continued, "good because when I'm out in public I tend to draw crowds."

I smiled and whispered, "So, do I," sashaying my way in front of him as if the shoes selection in Kaufmann's were running out of my size.

He grinned, watching with excitement as my hips and thighs fought for attention in my mini skirt.

Before long there was a crowd of individuals fighting for our date's attention and autographs. Dating a football player must be a never ending tug of war. As public figures everyone feels a sense of entitlement to them. My dad always stressed the need for me to know when to be a lady and when to be a freak. He would say that "men want women who know how to carry themselves and have confidence." He assured me that with these skills you can get a man to behave any way you want him to. This meant behaving like a lady in public even when the situation called for something else. The other part of this was being a freak. "Not every man is entitled to your cookies", he said sternly. "Most men only deserve your crumbs. Allow them to think they can get a piece of the cookie. Get what you need from them and be willing to drop a few crumbs here and there. Never leave a man stressed, and more importantly always leave any relationship on good terms, because you never know when you may need their ass to do a favor for you in the future." Words of wisdom that I quickly learned. Monica on the other hand, she as hood as they come and I don't understand, being she grew up in Tonawanda when Tonawanda was all white. Monica stood there causing a scene demanding that her date stop with the autographs and pay her attention. Me on the other hand, I walked away from the madness and continued shopping. After all I had an outfit to find for tonight and all this extra was something I did not plan on. I was putting my daddy's words of wisdom into practice.

About a half an hour later I heard some commotion coming from the store I was in. Soon the sales associate came to the dressing room and stated that "my boyfriend" would like for me to come out in the items that he chose. She handed me an armful of items. I noticed these items as I browsed the store. but due to my current wallet situation I decided not to bother falling in love with something out of my price range. So I did not grab them to try on. She smiled as if she knew a big commission was coming her way. I heard a male voice calling my name and asking me to come out of the dressing room. I smiled. It was a new, but familiar voice. I knew what he wanted to see and I really did need a second opinion on a few of these items. Being that I had lost Monica to her date, her opinion was void. I obliged. I walked out in a black tank style mini dress with a pair of strappy black and white tie up the leg stilettos. The dress hugged my hips and thighs like it was made for me. I chose a white, black and silver bracelet with the matching earrings. I pushed my hair behind my ears, so that the earrings would show. As I walked out the dressing room, there was a couple at the register cashing out their purchase. I heard the guy say damn, and saw his girl hit him. There was another guy watching me shaking his head as to give his stamp of approval. There were even a few ladies who paid me compliments on the way the dress looked. I made my way to my "boyfriend" as the young sale associate referred to him. He stood up eager with excitement and began to clap with approval. I twirled seductively and gave him a glance of the back of the dress, which was low cut semi- backless and exposed my bare back. I stood there and watched him look me up and down. I asked what he thought. He stated that he wanted to see more. I tried on about 7 more outfits all of which he had chosen for me to try on. With each outfit, I felt his anticipation growing. This cat and mouse game was just beginning and he had already begun to show me his hand.

The last outfit was a pair of lace black jeans with a lace crop top with a mock neck. It buttoned in the back. I cuffed the jeans and stepped into the peep toe red stilettos. I had my hoop gold earrings on with a nice gold bangle. I took the gold colored chain belt that I saw on one of the manikins and wrapped it around my waist. I freshened up my lip gloss with a slutty pout of red lipstick, tousled my hair, and took a glance in the mirror. Wow! I stood there admiring my curves and the way my body looked in this outfit. This was the outfit for tonight I thought. The sales person stated that the outfit was not even on the sales floor yet, I'm sure no one will be wearing anything like this tonight, so this was the one. I held on to the front of the shirt, I walked out of the dressing room, straight over to Mr. Cornerback , and asked him to button up the back of my shirt. His hands were strong, rough and soft at the same time. I moved my hair to the side, as he made his way down the back of the shirt with the buttons. I whispered, "Do I make you nervous?"

He laughed bashfully. As he finished buttoning my shirt, I walked away to the mirror in the middle of the store to get a final look at the outfit. The lace was placed perfectly over my nipples. Being that it was an unlined lace shirt I did not want to wear a bra and mess up the look of the outfit. Thank goodness the lace had some stretch to it. It hugged my 36DD's with the grace of grown man's hands. My breast are full and always at attention. My nipples were slightly erect from the air conditioned stored. I must have been admiring myself for a minute too long. A taller light skinned guy approached me. He tugged on the belt loop of the lace jeans and asked if he could have my number. He was cute and under any other situation I would have considered getting his digits and name. I politely pointed to my date and told him to ask him. He smiled and said maybe next time as he grabbed my hand and walked away. Mr. Cornerback sat patiently watching the stranger flirt with me. He waited for me to walk back over to him so he could get a better view. I stood there in front of him smiling. He stated "you're not wearing a bra."

"Does that bother you" I replied.

"No" he eagerly commented. Trying not to stare, but starring.

I stood there letting him capture every image of me. He asked, "who are you and where did you come from?" Staring each other in the eyes,

I replied" you wanna know that now or start with that over dinner tonight?"

"Dinner tonight with you wearing the red dress. Just you and I" he exhorted.

"Deal!" I took him by the hand and guided him back to the dressing room turned my back to him and asked if he would unbutton my shirt. When he finished he opened my dressing room door. I winked back at him and closed the door behind me. I quickly changed back into my mini skirt and top. Grabbed my coach bag, checked my makeup and freshened up with a dab of mango oil. I walked out of the dressing room to find Mr. Cornerback paying for everything I had tried on. The sales person was ringing up items that I knew were too expensive for my budget. "Wait a moment", "I can't..." before I could get another word in, Mr. Cornerback interrupted me and told me that he placed his card on file with the store. Any time I want something, all I needed to do was have them run the card. I told him that I could not possibly allow him to purchase these items for me. He stated that I did not have a choice, he liked what he saw and he was buying it. The sales lady rang the total up and to everyone's surprise my total came up to $5450. He stated is that it, as if a sigh of relief. Me on the other hand thought this nigga think he getting the cookies. The sales lady was as excited as she could be. By the time we were done she knew my name and everything. Even offered to make sure to call me once new items came in and hold them for me to try on. We left the store and with his black card, we conquered the mall. He getting to know me and me trying to figure out what this nigga's angle was.

Chapter Two

"Whatever You Want"
– Tony Toni Tone

"Whatever you want"- Tony Toni Tone

Anika

We finally made it back to Monica's house. Monica came from a working class family. She lived out in Tonawanda because it was closer to the plants her parents worked at. Monica lived in the middle of whiteville and acted anything but. She was my girl even though we did things differently. There was never any doubt, we had each other's backs no matter what. There were 4 of us that went and did everything together. Me, Monica, Yazz (Yasmine) and Ayanna. There were others that hung out with us, but when we talk about down for whatever, always about that life, sisters from another mister, us 4 were tight like that. Plus we respected the code. We never dated each other's ex's, and when we went out together we always left together no matter what nigga whispered in our ears. We always made sure that we made it home safe. Plus we kept each other's secrets and promised that we would never lie to each other or hold back anything good or bad. We were sisters, no blood, but in spirit and we held true to that.

"Hey Monica, who you talking too?", I asked.

"Ayanna and Yazz. I 2wayed them into the call. I was telling them about today and how they missed out... BIG!" Monica said rubbing it in. Monica hung up the phone. Monica told the ladies all about our day. Told them that we were going out to dinner and to be back at the house by 9:30 so that we could roll out to the club on time. Monica made plans with her baller. Because Mr. Cornerback had errands to do. He was sending a car to pick me up. Monica was heading out to dinner with her date. We showed each other all the goodies that were purchased for us. Monica had lingerie, sex toys and shit. I had clothes, shoes and purses.

"Damn Bitch, how you get him to trick-out on you like that?" she asked laughing. You gone give him some?"

"Girl you know me better than that. We having dinner and conversation, unlike your nasty ass", I said rolling my eyes. "And don't think I don't know that you been fucking this guy for a while now! Thanks for letting me know." I said as I went into the bathroom to take a shower.

Monica laughed. "Girl I fucked him day 1. Day 2 I sucked his dick so good he gave me the keys to the house and car. Day 3 that fool was giving me his credit card. I've been shopping all week!" she started laughing at her accomplishments.

I laughed too, for different reasons though. We were so different and so alike. My dad was right. If I did not respect myself then no one would.

I stepped out of the shower. Rubbed baby oil all over my wet body. I believe in air drying. I think the combination of baby oil and the air makes my skin so soft. My nails were perfectly manicured. My feet were soft and smooth and the toes shined in their deep red polish. It was 6:15 and the car Mr. Cornerback was sending over was due to arrive in 15 minutes. I slipped into my dress and had Monica zip me up. I put my earrings and bracelet on. I wore a thin gold necklace that adjusted in the middle forming a tassel. It hung effortlessly between my cleavage in this deep v neck red bandage dress that displayed the shape of my ass, child bearing hips and flat small waist. I chose the nude strappy sandals with the stiletto heels and a nude tannish colored clutch with a gold buckle. The dress stopped just shy of my knees, and was sleeveless. I picked up my tan colored wrap that he purchased to go with the dress just in case the restaurant was chilly. I finished my makeup but it was a hot humid 85 outside, I did not want the makeup to melt off. As I waited to air dry I spritzed myself with Victoria Secrets Rapture. Not only was I looking good and smelling irresistible, but I have a date. Something to take my mind off Quan. Besides, I planned on topping off the night with my girls, a few drinks and a DJ that was guaranteed to play my jams. We both took one final look in the mirror and gave each other our approvals on the outfits and out the door we went. I must have been looking ok, because I noticed Monica's man checking me out. But I didn't give him a second thought. Niggas like that are short lived. Little did he know.

Monica was gonna use and loose him before he even knew what happened. Two weeks tops and she would be on to the next. I walked over to the car Mr. Cornerback had sent for me. The driver greeted me with a smile and opened my door. I looked back at Monica to notice her opening her own door and jumping right in. The car drove off and all I could think about was what have I gotten myself in to.

We arrived at the restaurant. In all my days in Buffalo, I never knew this restaurant existed. It was located in the Old Statler Tower building. Now don't get me wrong, my mother was a debutant and so was I. My grandmother would not have had it any other way. It was the highlight of her year to be able to present me to the black elite society of Buffalo. She must have bought 20 copies of The Challenger newspaper just to show everyone how established she thought our family was. With that said, I was accustomed to eating out in fancy restaurants. My grandmother taught me proper etiquette. I can mingle with the best of high society. From art, ballet, classical music and theatre. I was exposed to the cultural elements of Buffalo. Not to mention, I am fluent in 4 languages and play the violin. Not bad for a girl who's grown up on the Eastside of the B-Low. I walked into the restaurant and was greeted by the hostess, "good evening Ms. Dumont, right this way" she stated. I followed her to a dim romantic setting located in the middle of the restaurant. There seated in a suit and tie was Mr. Cornerback. He stood to greet me and pulled my chair out. He leaned in and kissed my cheek.

"You look stunning" he whispered.

I blushed. "Thank you" I replied.

The waiter immediately bought over a bottle of wine and began pouring into the 2 crystal glasses on the table. All I could think was thank God they did not ask for my ID. Usually my body told whatever age men wanted me to be, but the truth was I had just turned 21. I had not updated my Driver's License yet and was probably still carrying around my fake ID with the name Deborah on it. Up until now, no one ever asked my age. The bouncers at the club were too busy flirting than checking the facts. So I had been Deborah, a fat white girl for years. It would have been embarrassing to pull that out of my wallet.

"What made you choose this restaurant?" I asked.

"It is one of the few places where I can have privacy. Everywhere I go people tend to want a piece of my time. I thought since you dealt with that earlier today, I could at least give you my full attention for dinner. Is this ok?"

"It's perfect" I said taking a sip of the wine.

"So, do you always make a habit of spending your money on complete strangers" I continued. "When and if they look like you maybe, but knowing how to be a lady gets you spoiled every time. You could have cut up like your girl, but you didn't. You play like you're not interested, but I know you are. You act like you don't know who I am. And I'm intrigued by that. So, tell me what makes you so special"- He inquired.

"I'm no different than the next girl. I'm only special because you don't know any different than the usual girls you date. While I appreciated your kind gesture this afternoon, I am more than capable of paying for my own items. I don't act a fool in public, causing scenes and being the stereotypical b-girl is not my thing.

As far as not knowing who you are, I know who you are. You play cornerback for the Bills, you were drafted in 1987 from a school in the Midwest. And last year you had 2 interceptions, 1 QB sack and 36 tackles. You have no children and you have a girlfriend last time that I check." I commented with a sly look on my face.

"Wow Ma, you did your homework, I'm impressed." He grinned as he took a sip of his wine. "I did my homework too. I happen to know that at least 4 of my teammates tried to kick it with you, but you turned them down. Your name makes for good locker room talk, made a few mutherfuckers jelly about tonight. A few told me that you and your girl aint nothing but trouble, you know all the fellas, be at all the parties and are connected. I also know your last 2 boyfriends were athletes. How did I do?" he asked jokingly.

"All wrong", I smiled admiring his dimples. "A lot of people know me and I know a lot of people especially men…can't help that. Your teammates couldn't come correct when they approached me, so no, they could not get any time. Locker room talk will be just that, talk. Have you seen any reason to think that I don't carry myself with respect and that kissing and telling with me is a no no? Plus what type of girl would I be if I ran through the Bills crew! Yes, I party, but I'm careful with whom, and lastly my last 2 male friends were average guys not ball players or rappers. I usually don't date athletes or rappers. And for the record I watch football, been a fan all my little life, so no real homework required. Now ask me what you really want to know?" I stated firmly but in joking tone.

"Why did you agree to have dinner with me?" he asked.

"Because you didn't flip when that guy came over to me when we were at the store and started flirting with me. It showed you had composure. That was different from how most guys in that situation would have acted. I thought it was cute. And so are you" I confidently answered.

"Don't get me wrong Pretty Lady, I was fuming inside. The way he was looking at you, pulling on you like that had me feeling some kind of way. I don't even know you and you got me looking sideways at dude. By the way what did he say to you?" He inquired acting macho.

"He asked for my number" I replied taking a sip of wine.

"Well" he questioned leaning back in his chair.

"Well what" I answered sarcastically.

"Come on Pretty Lady, I know you did not play me like that" he stated waiting for my answer.

"I told him to go ask you. If he wanted it badly enough he would have walked over to you and asked you if it was ok." I concluded as I stared into his eyes without blinking.

He laughed and said "definitely different, bold and cocky, cute with a fat ass and smarts to match. I think I like you Ms. Anika. I think I could get to love you if you keep this up!"

We laughed. It was nice. A good distraction from the heartache I was covering up. Besides what could be so wrong about dating a baller? Everything!

We finished up dinner and continued to get to know each other. He was handsome and playful. Nothing like to persona he displays on the field or I've read about in the paper or heard in the beauty salon. Today he was a gentleman. And for right now maybe that's what I needed, someone who could be a distraction for a heart torn. I told Mr. Cornerback about my plans for the remainder of the night. The look in his eyes told me he was hoping to continue the night together. The valet pulled up his

Range Rover. It was black with customer tinted windows and custom rims. He opened my door for me and helped me inside. He jumped into the driver's seat but not before tipping the valet for his services. He held my hand the whole ride back to whiteville. We pulled up to Monica's, he opened my door and helped me out. He hugged me and kissed me on my cheek. He told me to give him a call tonight to make sure I got in ok. I laughed and smiled as he let me go. I walked away knowing that his eyes were on my every move. With every switch of my hips, I know it pleased him. It pleased me and made me excited for the what if. I reached the back door turned to wave and off he drove.

Chapter Three

"Poison" – BBD

"Poison"- BBD

Anika

"Bitches!! Who the hell y'all supposed to be walking in here all did up and shit" Ayanna said as she high fived Monica and I as we entered the house.

Monica arrived at her home right before I did. From the look on her face and the tossed hair, I knew that her and Mr. Wide Receiver had sex. Nasty hoe! Ayanna wanted all the dirty details. And Monica would oblige sharing way too much about her conquest.

"Come on hoe's spill the beans, which Buffalo Bills yall two doing?" Ayanna asked laughing. "And why yall two always together when the good catches get reeled in" She said as she sat on the couch.

Monica filled in all the details. I went back in the bedroom and slipped out of my dress. I was standing in my bra and panties when Yazz came in with a glass of wine. Yazz was pretty. She has hair down to the middle of her back, she was thinner than me. I had a curvy frame, Yazz was thin, with legs for days. She had average size breast and a non- existent ass. But you couldn't tell her that her shit stank. She had attitude for days. She had these gorgeous hazel eyes that pierced your souls when she made eye contact with you. Dudes be all over my girl. They be all about them eyes. She has an exotic look. Usually when we go out, there is never any competition. No two of us look alike or are shaped alike. There is usually a dude tryin to get with each of us. We are so diverse that we offer something for every man out there. But Yazz was nasty. She would suck a dick in the back seat of a car and then turn around and go to church when she's done. In fact, I think she did just that in the church parking lot with one of the

Senior Pastors. That was her thing. Suckin dick. She was dick crazy. She would not fuck a dude unless she was serious about him, but she would suck a dick. And that turned dudes on. She got tricks for days. I've heard grown ass men cry after she sucked them off. Skillz, I know she got'em. Dudes say random shit like "your girl had me in tears", "I would spend it all on her". "That's a bad bitch you roll with." I just laugh, cause I'm sure that Yazz, Ayanna and Monica hear their fair share of shit about me. Mines is probably more fiction than fact though.

"So what we wearing tonight? I know yall bitches did not go to the mall and not cop us an outfit?" Yazz stated as she sipped on her glass of wine.

"Bitch you know me better than that "I stated as I threw a bag at her.

Just then Monica and Ayanna walk in. I tossed Ayanna a bag and Monica. They opened the bags like it was Christmas day.

"Bitch what! This is tight as fuck" Monica and Yazz said high fivin' each other.

Ayanna was too busy in the mirror looking at how the clothes might look on her. I got the lace outfit in assorted colors and styles. I choose the black outfit for myself. I bought the red lace shorts and long sleeve lace shirt for Yazz, Ms. Legs for day always wore red when we matched outfits. I got the blue lace mini skirt and halter top for Ayanna. Monica got the white lace capris with the matching tube top. Everyone got the same shoes, just different colors. We all got dressed each admiring the other in the mirror. The lace had the right amount of stretch that the outfits accentuated the right body parts of each of us. It was a panty and bra free kind of night. We were full of compliments and chatter. All ready to get our groove on. WBLK was jamming. We were singing and dancing tryna get in the mood for tonight. I must admit we looked good, but my body was booming! I looked just as good as I remembered in the store. We were ready to leave. The night was young and we were ready to party. Young and free. Not a care in the world. "Get Money!" we sang as we head out the door dancing and cheering the night ahead

We took the 30 min ride to the Falls. We took the I-90, jammin all the way. We got hyped off the music in anticipation of pitchers of long island iced teas and dudes admiring our fresh to def panty free outfits. Monica and Yazz smoked a blunt on the way there. I think every week I caught a contact high from that shit. Weed was not my thing. Both Ayanna and I did not smoke. My vice was sex. And not just any sex. But, fuck me hard and long, sweat out my hair, ride that dick like a cowgirl, in public make your toes curl sex. I loved dudes that could fuck my mind and body. If you could intrigue me mentally, my panties would get hella wet. I remember one time my tutor was explaining calculus to me and I finally got it. I got excited because I finally understood what the fuck the equation was asking me. I solved that shit and came on myself...hard. Made my tutor, an older college student touch my panties and then lick me dry. Needless to say, our tutoring sessions were a little more hands on after that.

We arrived just in time. The parking ramp was starting to fill up. We found a spot, hopped out, checked ourselves and then proceeded across the street to the Pleasure Dome. As we got closer we could hear the music pounding. The bass was so strong it felt like a heartbeat. On the way across, you saw several people in line all wanting to get inside and get their groove on. Me, I was ready. "Fuck that, I'm not waiting." I march my fine ass toward the beginning of the line. As we strolled by, we could hear dudes calling at us. I heard on guy say there she go, that bitch is bad. Another one reached for my hand and asked for me to save him a dance. One bold mutherfucker grabbed Yazz's ass and she turned around and grabbed his dick. Had him on his knees apologizing. Crazy bitch almost got left in that line. The bouncer who was crushin' on me was working the door. I whispered in his ear that

I would save a dance for him. He liked that. He was a big boy, mad cool, nothing to write home about. But he was always nice to me and if dancing one song with him moved me through that long ass crowded line faster it was worth it. The door opened, he stamped our hands and in we went.

The party was jumping. The DJ was on. It looked like half of Buffalo was in this joint. Yazz and Ayanna went to get drinks. Monica and I strolled the crowd tryna to see who was here tonight and who might be our next victims. Face down ass up by 2 Live Crew was being mixed into the song the DJ was playing. Me and Monica looked at each other and started laughing. I loved 2 Live Crew. Monica was just as nasty. The song came on and we headed to the dance floor. There were a few chicks on the floor but they were not doing anything special. There was this one guy, Monica grabbed him and started freaking the hell outta him. He turned toward me as if could handle both of us, so I joined in. Before long a crowd started to form around us as we freaked him like it was a dance threesome. I had my pussy all on his face as I grinded on him as he lay there humping Monica's face as she acted like she was giving him head. This dude had 2 friends that came on the dance floor to help him out, but they were no matched for us. We freaked them so hard I thought one of them had a wet spot on his jeans from bussin a nut. Besides, Yazz and Ayanna had arrived on the dance floor and we were gang bangin mutherfuckas left and right. Dudes were lining up to get freaked by us. Grinding and gyrating, it was like toxic sex on the dance floor under neon lights. We finally left the dance floor when the DJ started mixing in house music. Not my favorite genre, but I could dance to it. I made my way to the bar. The bartender Tony was a friend of my brother. He always looked out for me. He kept our drinks cold and safe from being

roofied. I gulped down that pitcher of long island tea as if there was no alcohol in it. As I was standing at the bar, I heard Monica scream with distaste "Who dat Bitch".

I turned around to see Quan walking in with some chick on his arm. Yazz and Monica rushed over there before I could even say a world. That's just what we do.

"This nigga done lost his fuckin mind, I'mma help him get it back" Monica said charging on a mission.

All I could see was Yazz and Monica going in on Quan and his chick. Yazz and Monica was in the girl's face. It got so heated that the girl ran off to the bathroom, only to be followed by Ayanna. A few minutes later, Ayanna came out with a hand full of weave.

"Damn bitch", Quan yelled. "What did you do to her?" he yelled out.

"Taught her ass a lesson" Ayanna replied. "Next time find a new spot to take your tricks" she laughed.

Quan rushed to the girl's side as she stumbled out of the lady's room. We made eye contact and I quickly looked away. He and that girl walked out the club just as quickly as he bought her ass in here. I could see Monica and Yazz egging them on, all before the bouncers had a chance to come break anything up.

"Take that raggedy ass bitch back to where you found her" Yazz laughed as she finished her drink.

I must admit, not the best way to handle that situation but that shit was funny. My bitches don't play. We a hunit all the time. Down for whatever. How ironic the DJ starts to play BBD- "I thought it was me". Yeah, I thought it was me too. A tear rolled down my face. I quickly wiped it off and took a sip of my drink. I headed back to the dance floor. There was no fun in crying over someone that didn't want you, and my daddy had taught me better that that. Fuck Quan and his new bitch.

The DJ was rockin' it. We stayed on the dance floor all night long. We were the main attraction tonight. Me and my girls gettin it in, showing the world our star status. Girls wanted to be us, guys wanted to get with us and all we cared about was having fun. When the DJ called out last round for alcohol, we knew the night was almost done. The Dome closed at 2am, but that did not mean the night was over. We took one more stroll through the club and made our way out the same door that kicked the party off tonight. As we walked out the nightclub the cool summer air washed over my body like a welcomed kiss. We piled out into the streets. All the DD's (Drug Dealers) were out flossin. Showing off their latest rides. Dudes stood leaning up against their cars tryna holla at the shorties that were coming out of the Pleasure Dome. It was almost like having your own personal radio playin. Every other car showed off their beats. Trunks were open displaying the amplifiers, speakers and whatever gadgets guys spend that paper on to make that bass go boom in their systems. Ayanna tapped me on the shoulder. As I turned see what was up, there stood Que. All "6'1 of his tall masculine frame. Quan aint have nothing over Que. Que made Quan look like a little kid, childs play. The only thing they had in common was the first letter of their names. Quan was supposed to be my turn with a good guy. And we all know how that shit turned out. Que was more good than bad in my eyes. Me and Que had history. He looked at me, smiled and signaled for me to here. Now my mind said no but my body screamed yes. That nigga had a hold on me and I aint never been his.

"Ooooohhh Bitch! you better go over there to that fine ass nigga and stop playin hard to get!" Ayanna and Monica teased as they clapped hands laughing.

Yazz joined in "That mutherfucka know he got you on wet! You better go over there and see what his ass want!"

I looked at them and rolled my eyes as I walked over to Que. He stood there in a pair of dark denim with a pair of cognac colored Timb's, with the cognac matching colored tee and ball cap on. He had on his signature platinum chain, with his initials medallion dangling at his chest. His left wrist was adorned with a Rolex watch that shined like the sun. I approached him in full b-girl attitude. I had to remain calm and collected. Couldn't have him thinking I was one of these dumb chicas' out here drooling for him.

"Hey Mami, what's up with you lady? A Nigga aint seen you in forever. You know you looking good. I'm liking them lace jeans, but I'm lovin that top" he said as he walked around me grinning and chewing on a Jamaican chew stick.

"I'm good Que." I replied tryna remain cool.

"I can see that. You aint got no love for you ya boy?" he questioned as he opened his arms waiting for me to enter for a hug.

I walked hypnotized into his arms and breathed in his air. It felt nice. Fuck that, it felt damn good. He held me with all the gentleness of a snowflake and warmth of a fireplace in winter. I could feel his heartbeat. I drank his cologne in and allowed it to bathe me. It felt good. He felt good and I did not want to let go. But I did. I backed up and caught my breath. We made eye contact and he was smiling a devilish grin. Our flirtation was rudely interrupted by some chick with cut off jean daisy dukes shorts on and a crop top. She had gold plated bamboo earrings, you know the ones they sale in Central Park Plaza at the Beauty Supply and Fashion Store. She walked over to him in true ghetto girl fashion and started questioning him.

"Who the fuck is this hoe? She questioned. "I know that you did not bring yo punk ass all the way up her to get caught out here talking to some fucking trick ass bitch!" she screamed at him pointing her finger in his face.

Que pushed that bitch out the way and went to grab for my hand. I pulled back and just stood there looking at him.

"Another time Que, another time" I stated as I shook my head and walked away. "Get ya girl before she gets hurt calling me out of my name," I calmly stated as I walked away.

Monica, Ayanna and Yazz all turned heads in the direction of all the commotion coming from my way. They were each posted up on some random nigga's ride. More than likely trying to make moves to hook up later tonight. They quickly went from sweet temptresses to hood rats ready to roll.

"What's up"- Ayanna spoke up.

"Girl, we good" I replied walking closer to the group of women I rode with.

I looked back to see that girl crying and pleading her case to Que. I don't know what she was saying but he wasn't hearing it. He pushed her aside as a stream of tears rolled off her cheek. Que and I made eye contact as we crossed the street headed back to the parking garage. I turned away. I knew all too well what that girl was going through. I felt bad for her. The only difference between her and me in that moment is no nigga is ever gonna have me crying and acting a fool in public. They aint never gonna see me hurt like that. Grown women cry in the dark and little girls wear their feelings on their sleeves. I guess by her actions Que and I both knew she wasn't woman enough for him.

Chapter Four

"I'm Dreamin"

– Christopher Williams

"I'm Dreamin"- Christopher Williams

Anika

Back on the I-90 head back to B-Low. Wow what a night. That punk ass Quan thought he was gonna stunt that bitch in front of me. And then running into Que. One more nigga from my past show up, I'll be convinced I'm in the twilight zone. As usual Monica is speeding down the highway. Blunts were being passed around in the car and the music was blasting.

We arrived at our second destination. The Touch of Trash... I mean the Touch of Class. This nasty ass hole in the wall club was located in the CP (Central Park) area of Buffalo. My girl Yazz was from the CP. Yazz knew every dude in this Hood. From the hustlers to the b-boys, all the gang bangers to the wanna bee's. CP was a middle class mostly black neighborhood at the time. Yazz came from a very professional household. Both her parents were investment bankers. They had worked their way up to Senior level management within their Firms. The minute that happened, they packed up Yazz and moved out to the suburbs. But that did not stop Yazz from hanging out in her hood. Her parents still owned their old house. They would rent the old house out to family. Yazz would use every excuse to stay at her old home. She said it kept her grounded being around people like her. She could not stand being around snotty ass white people. She would say "I don't skin and grin for no one". Yazz would spend the night at her old house during the week with relatives and on the weekend at her parent's house in Williamsville. When she turned 18 and graduated high school she moved into her old house on Jewett and has been there ever since.

The Touch as we referred to it was a bar with a dance floor. It had nowhere the amount of room of the Pleasure Dome. But what it lacked in room it more than made up for in Nigga's. All the ballers hung out here. Every drug dealer on this side of town copped a chair in this bar. It was an opportunity to come up on some money from a stunner that wanted to flex and trick out on a girl. With the right moves, a girl never had to pay for her own drinks in here.

All you needed to do was shake a little hip, pop that ass and walk with an attitude and the drinks would come rolling in. There was a small line outside of people waiting to get in. But not us. In true Yazz fashion she walked up to the front of the line, spoke to the bouncer and then whistled for us to come on. The bouncer stamped our hands and in we went. The touch was packed. There was a table empty all the way in the back of the dance floor. We grabbed that table and took a seat to survey the room. The bar was dimly lit. The only thing you could see was the strobe lights echoing off the mirrored wall on the dance floor. The DJ was alright. People were dancing and having a good time. We noticed a few ballers checking for us, but it was too early to try to be claimed. The DJ began to play some reggae. All I know was my hips began to sway back and forth as the pace of the song increased. Ayanna stood up and screamed "this is my jam!" as she headed to the dance floor. We all followed suit. The rhythmic sounds of Junior Reid's "One Blood" was humming through the speakers. It was almost like a trance, or a voodoo curse had been cast on me. I got lost in the music and my body began to roll and grind and flex its way into the islands. I started rolling my ass and hips like I was a Trini gal. I moved seductively to the sounds making eye contact with myself in the mirror. I touched my body admiring myself in the mirror. Slow and precise hip movements followed by fast rolling of the waist and then slow again. Breaking it down to the floor and then back up again. Slow, fast, tight whines of the hips, with pops of ass movement. I was becoming drunk off my own sexiness. I could see how men get turned on by women dancing. This shit is fucking hot!

The DJ picked up the pace by mixing in Shabba Ranks Ting-A-Ling, and the crowd went wild. My hips didn't miss a beat. Nothing spoke to me more than reggae music. It was sexual. It was innocent, and troubled all at the same time. As the song progressed a Jamaican dude approached. With towel in hand he came for me. He slid his leg in between my thighs and started to grind me as our bodies moved in unison. I kept up with his every stroke. My hips and waist moved in patterns that mimicked a dancehall queen. Most guys thought I was from the island being I'm fluent in French and the way I dance. I wasn't afraid to get nasty and allow the music to move me. It was freedom. Mentally, sexually and spiritually. We moved as if we were one person. I rolled my hips and he was there to catch them. We went low and high, we sexed on the dance floor. I could feel his manhood pounding against me, begging to be freed of this torture. Our session was interrupted only by the buzzing of his pager. He kissed my hand, winked and departed our exchange. Not one to be undone, Monica was grinding her ass on some dude as he stood against the wall and she worked her magic up and down his manhood. The look on his face was pleading for her to come home with him. She danced slow and hard, winding her hips and popping her ass. She served him from the front with one leg up and he gave it to her from the back as if it was doggy style. She moved with all the control of a wild animal and as I looked around, dudes were watching her waiting for a turn for her to fuck them on the dance floor. Ayanna was nestled between 2 guys as they shared her hips and ass as she worked them hard. She had one guy's head in her hands and pushed him down to her garden while grinding her hips and as if he was drinking her juice. The other guy was busy kissing all over her neck as he held onto her hips as she pushed her ass out to him to rub his dick on. She would turn from front to back, allow each of them an opportunity to excite her senses. Yazz had a nigga on his back on the floor riding him as if she was a cowgirl. He picked her up with her legs wrapped around him and allowed her to roll her hips on him as he stood still. She was fucking him dry. The intensity to which they were dancing, one would have easy thought they were really fuckin'.

The DJ kept the reggae going. He was mixing in some Buju Banton- "Boom Bye Bye". The crowd just swayed in a trance. I was back at the mirror with my eyes closed allowing the music to control me. I felt someone approach from behind. His movement was all too familiar. He got low enough for me to sit on his lap as I gave him my ass in quick ticking motions. I leaned back into him and allowed him to hold me. He started kissing my neck as our bodies became twisted in the song. I did not need to open my eyes. I knew there was only one person that my body would allow me to give into like this. Que. He rocked my body like an ocean's wave. I gave him all of me. The pain I was carrying from my heart being broken by Quan, the stress of school and work and me being mad at him for allowing that girl to interrupt us and deny me his company. I released all that and more onto him and he openly accepted my gift with every movement he made. Chaka Demus & Pliers "Murder she wrote was playing in the background. We picked up the pace. Parted just enough for him to stroll up to me the way guys do when approaching a girl when reggae is playing. He waved his towel in the air and let out a call, and the club went wide. He slid his leg in between my thighs and I began to tick my hips all over his leg. Rolled my back all the way back and ticked my ass and hips all over him. He took me low and high. He grabbed my leg and put it around his neck and there I stood one leg in stilettos ticking my waist and hips to the beat on him. He held me tight and I served him well. We were in our own zone. No one else in the world. When we came to, there was a crowd starting to form around us as we danced. Our sexing on the dance floor was starting to arouse others as they watched in awe and pure satisfaction and approval of our moves. The DJ was on a role. The last of the reggae songs he played for the night was Supa Cat- Don Dada. With a crowd watching, I decide to give them what they wanted and give Que another reason to want this. Up against the mirrored wall I did my signature head stand and facing him, eyes closed began to work my magic, casting spells on all those watching. Monica, Yazz and Ayanna joined in. There we were serving up ticks, hips and ass, moving our waist to the beat of Supa Cat. With each hip movement I watched him eye me. I watched Que sway with my moments. I saw him grab his manhood as if it were me. He was turned on and I loved every bit of how my dancing was making him want me. I was turned on and needed him to release my sex and help me pray my worries away. I wanted him to follow my hips into the warm waters of the Caribbean. I wanted Que to see me make love to the air and allow him to bask in the sweet scent. There I stood upside down on the dance floor fucking myself, making him dance to my rhythm. I wanted to open my eyes to see him watch me. But to my surprise, when I opened my eyes and stopped being lost in the song, Que was gone. That nigga was gone. He was nowhere to be found.

Chapter Five

"I Wanna Make Love"
–Lilo Thompson

"I wanna Make Love"- Lilo Thompson

Anika

We arrived back at Monica's house after a wild night of partying. With all that dancing I was surprised that my hair had not completely sweated out. I was still sour after being stood up on the dance floor by Que. I should have never allowed myself to fall victim to that bull shit. Everyone had made plans for the night. Monica was about to go kick it with a guy named Jerome. He was some up and coming rapper from NYC. He did a few cameos on a few artist tracks and was hot on the underground circuit. They met a few weeks back and he was in town. Monica said she was going to fuck him so good that he would rap a whole song about how good her pussy was! We all laughed at the thought. Ayanna and Dade was hookin' up for the night. No matter how many times we told her to stay away from those crazy ass Jamaicans, she kept finding them. Ayanna loved Dade and I know he cares about her too. They both too damn stubborn and are cut from the same grimy ass cloth. They may see other people, but at the end of the day they always found their way back to each other. Sometimes crazy attract crazy, and crazy like them two only result in trouble. And the two of them together was a whole lot of crazy and trouble waiting to happen. Yazz had a booty call with a nigga named Jay from CP. He and Que were like brothers. If there was anyone that Que trusted Jay would be at the top of the list. He was street, but he carried himself differently from most dudes that hung around Que. He was hella smart. I could tell that his past did not match his present situation. But he was made cool. And I liked the way he treated my girl, unlike his counterpart Que.

No sooner than we closed the door to Monica's house, there was a parade of niggas standing outside waiting to sample the sweet honey they longed for after a night of visual pleasures. After watching us on the dance floor or lusting after our contoured physiques in our semi see through clothing, they were ready to dip their hands in the honey jars. The ladies were so eager to get their freak on that no one noticed that I had not made plans. I was cool with that. Needed some time to get my head right anyway. As they were making sure I was going to be ok, I assured them I would be, there was a knock on the door. Monica yelled "Motherfuker if yall don't wait a goddamn minute" thinking it was one of their booty calls. The doorbell rang. Ayanna annoyed rushed to the door and opened it wanting to give them a piece of her mind. To her surprise the door was not for any of them. "Well, I guess you won't be so alone after all" Ayanna sarcastically said grinning ear to ear as she opened the door to welcome in my guest.

"What are you doing here?" I asked with a puzzled look on my face.

"You never called to let me know that you made it home ok. I see you wore the lace outfit tonight. You look just a sexy as you did when you tried it on. I'm sorry ladies, did not mean to interrupt, I was just getting ready to head home and thought I'd stop to make sure Anika was ok"- He said not taking his eyes off of me.

"Girl you gone be ok?" Yazz asked as they all headed to the door.

"Yes. I'm sure I'm in good hands now" I said waving goodbye to my girls. "In fact, we out too!" I stated as I grabbed Mr. Cornerbacks hand and closed the door behind us

He drove the 30 minutes back to his house. I sat there in the car thinking about the night's events. The mix of emotions that hang over me. Allowing myself to be vulnerable was never my strength. Hell, it isn't even a weakness. My father had taught me all too well the ways of the street and being vulnerable was not a trait I could afford. Letting my guard down without just cause was a foreign concept. Everything I did was an orchestrated play. I did not move unless I could deal with the outcome.

Even now. Me in the car with this man at 4:23am could only mean one thing. With the week I had and especially after tonight, I needed to release some stress. I needed to feel appreciated and valued even if it was temporary. At least I could control this outcome. I was at least willing to play this game knowing all the cards were on the table. There would be no feelings, no emotions, no baggage, no history. Just sex. Sex and nothing else.

I sat in the living room of his mini mansion, admiring his masculine decor. Mr. Cornerback was in the kitchen fixing drinks.

"Red or White" he asked

"Neither" I replied. "I'm a hard liquor kind of girl. I'll take some whiskey or brandy if you have it. Bring the bottle!" I said jokingly.

"Wow Ms. Lady, It's like that"

"It's like that" I replied.

He entered the room with a bottle of Jack and a bottle of Christian Brothers with 2 shot glasses. I could hear the smooth sounds of baby face playing in the background. He must have surround sound. It was low enough to go unnoticed, but once you hear a Babyface song playing it instantly relaxes you. I took a shot of Jack and a quick shot of Christian Bros. I asked to use the bathroom. I walked down the dimly lit hallway and into the second door on the right. I needed to get out of my clothes. It felt like I was wearing a layer of sweat and lust from dancing my cares away. I took off my shirt by pulling it over my head. I unzipped my lace jeans and allowed them to fall to the floor.

There I stood free. No bra and no panties. I never wore panties. They were just as uncomfortable as wearing a bar to me, plus they gave you those unsightly panty lines in your clothes. I stood there admiring my body in the mirror. My makeup was still flawless and I still smelled of Victoria Secrets Rapture. I walked back into living room naked. I walked right over to him. I stood there watching him look at me. I could see the shadow of my curves cast on the wall from the candles that were flickering around the room. I grabbed the bottle of brandy, and with the top off began to pour it down the front of my body. It was cold and refreshing. I took a sip of the brandy from the bottle and watched as Mr. Cornerback approached me with the eagerness a kid on his birthday with me being his present. He licked and kissed the brandy that dripped off my body. I poured more and watched him get intoxicated from the shots of sex that awaited him as he caressed my body, drinking alcohol off me. I placed the bottle back on the table. I could hear R. Kelly coming from the surround sound. My body began to move to the beat.

Watching him, I danced. Rolling my hips touching myself to his and my pleasure. I turned so that he could get a better view of my ass as it clapped to the chorus of the song. I bent down and stretched my body in ways that resembled a contortionist. I was thick and flexible. My years in classical dance were finally paying off. I moved slow, sweet, innocently, yet everything we were about to do was anything but. I watched as he looked on in amazement. I saw the bulge in his pants grow with anticipation of having me. I walked back over to him and placed myself on his lap straddling him. I danced facing him as he began to kiss the taste of brandy off my nipples. I stood up placing my neatly trimmed pussy in his face. Allowing him to devour me as he cuffed my ass and pushed me into his mouth. He talked to me using his tongue. He spoke languages that I had not mastered yet. I was learning as he held me by my ass and picked me up and ate me like a piece of watermelon. I wrapped my legs around his neck as my body rocked back and forth. I was now speaking his language and he mine. His tongue sang the most beautiful song to me. I danced and he sang and in a moment of pure ecstasy we sang a chorus together that mimicked an Ashford and Simpson tune. I unwrapped my legs from his neck freeing him from my bondage. I sat on his lap back facing him as my body moved to the lyrics of the next song. I rolled my hips as he held me and kissed my back. I could feel his manhood aggravated at the cruelty of not being able to enter me. I unzipped his pants as I existed my carnival ride. I sat there on the couch as he stood and removed his clothing. I watched his every movement. Body parts that mimicked sculptures crafted by an artist. Solid muscles, defined, hard and made in God's image. His dick hung heavy at the overdue introduction of me. It was pretty. It was long. And just like him it was thick.

My pussy wettened with the thought of experiencing this journey with him. He picked me up off the couch. With my legs wrapped around his waist, I allowed him to enter me. I sighed with relief. I rode him as if I was on a journey. His dick filled every crevice in my garden. I rode him. I wanted him. I held on tight as he bucked back giving me the hard beats of his drum. He held me leaving his fingerprints planted deep into me. We fucked right there in the front room, in front of the big beautiful bay window as the streaks of light beam cascaded across the sky. The sun was rising and so was our sex.

Chapter Six

"You Don't Have To Worry"

–En Vogue

"You Don't Have To Worry"- En Vogue

Anika

It was Sunday and all I wanted to do was relax. I managed to release some unwanted stressed and landed myself a whole new wardrobe. What a weekend. I managed to leave Mr. Cornerback early this morning. He held me hostage with his sex. It was late Saturday afternoon when I finally woke. I was greeted by the delicious aroma of bacon. I put on one of his wife beater tees went into the aux suit in the bedroom. It was massive. I thought to myself a girl could get use to this. There was a double sink, surrounded by granite countertops. The walk-in shower was big enough to hold a party in. There were water jets all over. Just thinking of the power of the sprays made my muscles relax. The whirlpool tub set nestled up under a picturesque window that overlooked the backwoods of the property. I quickly located a washcloth and towel and made my way into the shower.

I dried off and put back on the tee shirt. I washed my hair and had the towel wrapped around my hair as if I was an African Queen. I walked out the bedroom and down the hall to the kitchen.

"Good afternoon" I said watching the star football player play chef.

"Good Afternoon Ms. Anika. I hope I did not wake you". He smiled.

I smiled, not noticing that we had company. There stood a few of his teammates. They had been talking about the new playbook and the upcoming season. They all stopped talking when I walked in the room. I could tell they were admiring the way his tee shirt hugged my curves. I could model anything and give it life. Luckily the tee shirt was just long enough to cover my ass cheeks… barely. He walked over to me and hugged me tight. His embrace was welcomed. I took the towel off my head and allowed my damp now curly hair to hit my shoulders. They watched in awe. He signaled for his friends to leave. I stood there waving goodbye as one of them said Damn!!!!

After we were done eating we lay in the bed. I was relaxed. I was stress free for once and I knew that I wanted him. So, I took him again.I think my overactive aggressive sex drive had him on full. I took him again and again.

We took a break only to eat dinner. I finally told him that I need some fresh air. He obliged and we ended up at the only place that would truly make a girl happy. Back at the mall. I told him that it was 5:45pm and the mall was set to close at 6:00pm.

"Listen Ms. Anika, you gonna have to trust that I know what I'm doing" he winked and opened my car door. He took my hand and led me to the store. They we waiting for us. He had called ahead and paid for select stores in the mall to stay open.

"Yesterday you seemed like you had a long week. I thought that if I ever get another chance to make you smile. I'm going to take it. The mall is yours." He explained as he sat down and sipped the champagne that the sales clerk served in the fluted glasses.

Store after store he spoiled me. He bought things he liked on me, things I liked and everything in between. I had Victoria Secrets, Lord & Taylor, Cache' and more. There were shoes, lingerie, dresses, tops and accessories. He gave it all to me. I normally would not indulge in this type of behavior, this is usually Monica's thing. Niggas trickin out on me never impressed me. But this was different.

After shopping we went back to his house. He took the bags and placed them in his closet. I asked what he was doing. He said "this is for when you decide to come back over. I'll keep the things I liked for here. Everything else you can take with you" he grinned. I loved is confidence. He hung the items in the walk-in closet. It was starting to look like his and hers. I had to remind him that this was only day 2. He laughed.

"What is your girlfriend going to think about this?" I asked folding my arms with attitude.

He grabbed my hands and said, "why you worried about her when I'm here with you? Huh?"

"I'm with you. Truth… We broke up. She did not like being in Buffalo. Said she missed Miami. Couldn't handle sharing me with the fans. So, she left. And I let her. So you see Ma, the only clothes I'm hanging up is yours. After last night and today, I'm thinking I know what I want. I'm just waiting for you." he said as he finished hanging up my clothes.

We sexed some more. We explored every inch of his mansion. My sexual conquest of him took him around the world and we didn't even leave the state. After all that excitement I was happy to be back in my own bed. Rested. I hung up my clothes. Even checked in with the girls to fill them on the rest of the weekend. They caught me up on all the action I missed Saturday at the Sweet Waters. They even told me that Quan was there. He seemed to be lookin' for you. Asked Ayanna where you were. She just said she didn't know. I could not think about Quan right now. I was too busy thinking of Mr. Cornerback. He had introduced a new player to the game and I wanted to suit up and play my position.

Chapter Seven

"Tonite" – DJ Quick

"Tonite"- DJ Quik

Monica

"Puff, puff pass nigga" I said demandin' the blunt back. I was on top of Jerome straddling his dick like a professional bull rider at the rodeo. He passed the blunt back and I took a toke, inhaled, held it and then blew out. The room was filled with the aromatic scent of sex and ganja. It was the combination of my high and his hard dick that encouraged me to fuck him hard. The headboard to the hotel bed banged against the wall as I bucked on his hard cock. I was up on my feet squatting on his stiff rod, riding him like the red cape of a Spanish matador had waved me on to the finish. Without losing my rhythm I took another puff of the la and passed it back to Jerome. He puffed and so did I. I climbed down from my ride and began to smoke his dick like it was a blunt. With every stroked I made with my hands, it was as if I rolled the perfect blunt. I sucked his blunt as is it was the best weed in the world. I could taste the sweetness of my pussy on his dick as I puffed. I took him deep down my throat, causing me to gag giving way to wet sounds from choking on his massive long dick. It scraped my throat as I blew it long and deep with continuous motions sliding up and down, and up and down. I would bring my month back up his shaft with all the juice my mouth could produce. I would blow on it as if to keep the weed lit. Spitting on it I would pretend I was using my tongue to seal the ends of his dick creating a perfect seal along his vein that ran up and down the center of his cock. It was magical, the way I made Jerome's eyes to roll back in his head and toes crack.

That's what I wanted. To please him and do what other girls were not willing to do. I enjoyed every moment of having his dick in my mouth. It gave me power. I loved being able to command men with my mouth. I knew that if I blew, I could get whatever I wanted from a man. Sucking dick was just part of the experience of being with me. There were only 3 things that turned me on. Dick, Weed and Money, and not necessarily in that order. I puffed the blunt and got high. I paused as I jerked his dick with my hands. I managed to keep it lubricated by allowing my saliva to drizzle on the head of his dick. I took my tongue and made circular motions as the spit wrapped around the his shaft. I was the band conductor and his dick was my wand. Every bit of my dick sucking skills was musical and magical.

"Ahhhh" he screamed with excitement.

"Yeah boy, Mo make that dick real hard!"

"Yeah Mo, do that shit baby, I got you Mo, Daddy got you girl" he whispered.

"You got me Daddy! You got me good. I make Daddy wanna come all over my pretty face? What daddy gone give me for that pretty face?" I questioned taking all of him into my warm mouth. I sucked him slow and hard with deep strokes. Thrusting my head into his lap as if bobbing for apples. Each time going deeper and deeper to achieve my goal.

"Anything Mo, Anything!" scream Jerome as he let out aloud demanding grunt!

That was just what I wanted to hear. I released my grip on his dick, taking him out of my mouth just in time. He sprayed his sweet juice across my face. The thick and shiny lotion that came from deep within him, now cover me like water from the shower. His body shook in exhausted pleasure. He watched as he squirted his seed all over my face. He sat in awe as I caught his juice with my mouth and tongue. What I could not catch I grabbed with my hands and placed in my mouth. Once he was done, I took the collection and spit back onto his dick and gently sucked it off. I did this about 3 times each time making sure to rub the lotion back onto him with my mouth. Massaging his dick with his seed and continuing to blow the cool air causes a tingling sensation that made his body shake. When I was finally done I drank whatever was left. I did not miss a drop.

"I want the car" I confidently stated with a straight faced.

"Done" he relinquished. As his body lay there exhausted and satisfied.

I smiled, "Shit Monica you a bad bitch" I thought to myself. A bad bitch indeed.

Chapter Eight

"A Bitch Iz A Bitch"
– NWA

"A Bitch Iz A Bitch"- NWA

Monica

The doorbell rang, I wasn't sure who it could have been. It was too early to be Ayanna, Yazz or Anika. Hell, we just left each other only hours ago.

"Buzz, Buzz" went the doorbell.

"Who the fuck at my door?" I screamed out the kitchen window.

"Monica, it's me, Terrence, come let me in", a familiar voice cried.

Damn Terrance! This nigga been sweatin' me for weeks. Gave his ass some head and this nigga tryna wife me up. I aint got time for his punk ass right now. I barely got any sleep. I left the hotel at about 9am, Dropped Jerome off at the airport, so I could keep his truck. After my performance last night, he could not deny me. I get to ride around in his car for the next 2 weeks. Bitches everywhere gone know I got that nigga on lock.

I walked to the side door and let Terrence in. He went in for the kiss and I did not have the strength to push him back or block the kiss. At this moment it was easier to allow him to taste Jerome's cum on my lips and tongue. He came in carrying a bag of goodies. He walked straight down into the basement sat down on the couch and opened the first of many bags. He sat 2 white take out platters on the table. He had gone to GiGi's and picked up breakfast on his way to see me. He was preparing the coffee table as if we were at the restaurant. He patted the couch cushion next to him as if to say come sit by me. I obliged. Hell, I had worked up a hell of an appetite after everything that went down last night. I sat and opened the container and went in. I ate the pancakes, bacon, eggs and home fries. He handed me a kid size Styrofoam cup of orange juice. Terrence was taking his time eating. All I wanted to do was sleep. And now that I had some food in my stomach I was ready to be down for the count. The only thing that was missing from the moment was a blunt. So as he finished working on his home fries and bacon, I pulled the album cover from up under the tv console, pulled the bag of weed out my bra, took the last dutchy out the pack and began to remove the old filling and replaced it with the new. Just as I was licking my perfectly wrapped blunt, the doorbell rang. What the fuck? With blunt on the table I rushed up the stairs annoyed at whomever was messin' up my vibe. I opened the door and there stood Mike. I laughed. This is going to be interesting I thought.

"Sup girl, I saw you last night at the club, was tryna get at you but it looked like some utha niggas all up on you, and you know me, I don't block anybody from doin' them. Ya know" Mike said tugging on my tee shirt.

"I saw you kid, but you know me" I replied

"Yeah I know you shorty" he paused as he leaned in closer and whispered" I know you real well."

I blushed. "So what's up nigga you tryna come in or just stopped by say what's up?"

Mike stood there with this devilish smile on his face. This nigga was fine was as hell. He was a real thug nigga too. Snatch a bitch by the ponytail and beat her pussy up kinda thug. He stood "6'0" even and was deep dark chocolate in complexion. He was tatted up and always sported a NY logo hat. He was from the Bronx. So his accent was thick. He stood there waiting for me to invite him in. Looking at me with those big brown eyes.

In a very playful tone I explained" I have company right now, and…"

I was cut off abruptly

"You got feelings about this nigga?" he asked "What y'all doing?"

"Nothing much, about to smoke this blunt and get high as fuck!" I laughed. "And shit you know me I aint catchin feelings about nobody, only thing I'm chasing is money, dick and weed. If a nigga aint got one of the 3 he can't fuck with me" I said bluntly.

"So let me in" he said steppin' even closer to me.

I let Mike in and we headed down stairs. I introduced Terrance to Mike. It was awkward, but fuck it. It wasn't the first time 2 of my niggas was in the same room with each other. I sat back on the couch in my spot, picked up the blunt lit it and took a puff. Mike and Mario was eyeing each other. All I could think about of was they better not start fighting in my shit. Besides Mike would beat Terrence's ass to a pulp. I puffed again and laughed at the thought. I offered up my blunt to whomever was next. Terrence passed. Goody tu shue ass nigga, I forgot he didn't smoke. So I handed it over to Mike. As he puffed, Terrence broke the silence and asked Mike, "So how you know Monica?"

"Me and Mo go back. I've been knowing her fo years" Mike explained

"Know Monica like how?" Terrence insisted.

"Mike knows my cousin "B". They grew up together in the "Boogie Down". I would visit during the summers when I was younger, now Mike lives here." I puffed.

"Besides, now Mo's all grown up and I've gotten to know her in other ways" Mike said then puffed and blew in Terrence's direction.

I could tell Terrance was starting to feel some kind of way. I only fucked with Terrence because I was bored. He had been flirting with me for some time. Against my better judgement I went on a date with him. One thing lead to another and we ended up back at his house. We fucked. And from the way this nigga been acting, I must have been the best damn thing since sliced bread to him. He been sending me flowers, giving me money, showing up with food and cleaning my place. This nigga had it bad, even though I told him that I was not looking for anything serious. He keeps on tryin. Poor sap, told him I was no good and this fool keep tryna wife me. Change me. But he gone learn.

Mike and Terrence was exchanging dirty looks as I continued to puff and get mesmerized in cloud of relaxation that we were covered in.

"Damn yall niggas trippin!" I said laughing out loud.

Mike moved from the love seat over to my right side on the couch. I was now right in the middle of Terrence and Mike. Me and Mike continued to puff. With each interaction between me and Mike, Terrence grew more and more upset. I decided to loosen the mood. I grabbed Terrence and kissed him. I grabbed Mike and kissed him. I was embracing my high and just wanted to relax. What I really wanted was to go to sleep but these 2 rude ass niggas had already messed that up for me. So the next best thing was dick. I kissed Terrence again. I kissed Mike again. The only person that wasn't enjoying himself was Terrence. He was killing my vibe. As I was trying to get Terrance to loosen up, Mike pulled me to him and started kissing me.

"What the fuck Monica, how you just gonna sit here and do this shit?" Terrence angrily spoke standing up.

"Nigga sit yo ass down. You can sit the fuck down and join in, you can watch or you can get gone. What you aint gone do is stop me from being me" I said upset that this nigga was actin up.

"You supposed to be my girl and you sitting up her acting like a hoe. Bringing this nigga up in here in my face disrespecting me like this, what the fuck Monica" cried Terrence.

I was feeling real bad about how this was about to go down. But this nigga had been warned.

"Look here nigga! I told you what I was about when we hooked up. I told you I wasn't looking for a commitment. I told you I was not that kind of girl. But you kept coming back. You the one tryna play house and shit acting all emotional. If we in a relationship than you my bitch. You cookin', cleanin', crying and shit. Nigga I sucked yo dick, I didn't walk on water or turn shit to wine and you acting like I'm God. Back the fuck up! What you think, you the only dick I've sucked? You kissed me this morning and I had another nigga's cum on my breath. Now what nigga? Fuck you!"

Terrence stood there with tears in his eyes. I had broken that man down and gave him a dose of reality. In my world I'm the Alpha and Omega and aint nobody ever gonna stop me from gettin mine.

"You gone join in or you gone get the fuck out?" ... I paused ... "In fact don't answer that the both of yall get the fuck outta here and let me get some rest!" I screamed.

They both looked at me and headed up the stairs and out the door.

"You know what Monica, you aint nothing but a bitch!" Terrence screamed as he stumped off looking like a sad as nigga.

Mike smiled and said "I'll get at you later Mo" looking at ole boy shaking his head.

'Whateva nigga" I replied with a stale attitude.

A.A. LEWIS

Damn now I'm horney and sleepy. FUCK!!

Chapter Nine

"Queen Of The Pack"
– Patra

"Queen of the Pack"- Patra

Ayanna

Me and Dade stopped off at the store on the corner E. Delavan and Durham before heading back to his spot. He needed to take care of something before we called it a night. We pulled up to the corner. Even at 4:30am in the morning niggas was standing guard. There must have been at least 6 mutherfuckers out there waitin' and watchin'. Dade jumped out the Jeep and pulled me along with him. I followed closely behind him as he entered the store. The store smelled of incense and curry. The store was full of island essentials. They showcased all the latest and some classic reggae cassettes. They offered body oils and the original Shea Butter. But what they were known for was their authentic Caribbean cuisine. The brother behind the counter had just prepared a batch of beef patties and placed them in the table top food warmer. I was looking around as Dade went into the back of the store with one of the dudes that was standing guard outside. I got some beef patties and coco bread. They had the best beef patties this side of NY. Everything about the store was authentic. Dade said it was like having a piece of home right here in Buff. On Tuesdays they severed curry oxtails with peas and rice and niggas within a 10 block radius was lining up for a plate. Me, I was more of a roti gal. But I knew anything sitting around this hour of the night was not fresh and I could not afford to have my stomach acting crazy. So beef patties it was. The guy went ahead and bagged my food. I threw a pack of cherry and grape chew sticks in the bag and walked back to the Jeep. Being with Dade, I never had to pay. No matter where we went and what I wanted, with Dade it was mine. People would just bag shit up and hand it to me or take it out to the car.

Everyone knew I was Dade's main girl. When I was with him girls would stare and guys would look away. No one ever came out their mouth wrong at me. There was this one time when we were together at a restaurant having dinner when this female marched up to our table demanding Dade tell her who I was. I remember she had tears in her eyes. She was cute, and had a nice shape. She sported micro braids that went straight down her back. She started causing a scene. I just sat there drinking my glass of wine. I knew no matter what happened, Dade was not going to let anyone come for me. He signaled for his peeps to come in and get her. They apologized and removed her from our site. Dade excused himself from the table and went outside to handle his business. He came back in and apologized, kissed me and ordered a bottle of Cristal. After that instance I knew that I was his main bitch.

I sat in the car like I was being protected by the Secret Service. There were Jamaicans all over that corner. Dade came out gave dap to a few of his peeps and off we drove. Dade lived between Lisbon and Parkridge. He owned several properties in the city. He even put a few in my name. Said anytime I wanted to stop playin Miss Independent I could come live with him. Like that was ever gonna happen. As much as I loved me and Dade together, we both did too much dirt. I knew he fucked other women. And he knew I did other guys. As long as we did not flaunt that shit in each other's faces all was good. We made a pack not to disrespect each other that way. Fucking was one thing, but there was to be no outside rendezvous with other people. He would say "Wooman, yuh da only one farr me, I doun care who you wit as long as yuh hart belong to me" he would say in a deep island accent. It's a good thing I kept my dirt on the low, because if this crazy ass fool ever found out about me and the dudes I be kickin it to on the side, we would all be dead.

He parked the car in the garage and in we went. The house smelled of vanilla beans and coconut. I'm thinking it was incense from the store we just left. His house was decorated like a bachelor pad. The living room had a futon couch and 2 leather club chairs. In the middle of the room stood a big screen size floor model TV. There were no pictures on the wall no plants hanging around. He had 2 book shelves, one in each corner of the room that anchored the futon. There was a dining room, but no table, no chairs. The kitchen was small, but I'm sure I could cook some really good meals in it. The bedroom was where all the excitement happened. There was a round king size bed located in the middle of the room. The headboard was a velvet royal blue with pin tucks. There was a dresser that held up the tv and stereo. He took my hand and lead me to the bedroom.

Dade liked to undress me. He took his time as if he was examining my body like a doctor. Once my clothes were all off, he undressed. We then moved to the bathroom. He ran the water and filled the bathtub up with bubbles and hot water. The room smelled of jasmine and cloves. He stepped in first and guided me in after him. He sat down and allowed me to rest my back on his chest. He kissed me gently. I sat there relaxing in his arms, as the water filled the tub and the bubbles covered me like rose petals. He washed me. Starting with my neck. He moved the washcloth down my back and onto my butt. He rubbed the soap into my skin and then rubbed his body into mine. I could feel his massive love stick growing with each glide across my skin. As he approached my thighs, he opened me up by lifting my left leg and placed it on the rim of the tub. He caressed my thighs by kissing away the day's activities. Deeper and deeper he drove his lips, until he reached my petite fleur. It was like the sweet scent of my garden had drove him to me. He kissed and I moaned. He continued to kiss and drive me into him. I stood there watching him devour me, allowing him to cleanse my insides and wash away my fears. The way his tongue peeled away my layers, the way his tongue planted seeds of satisfaction, the way his lips parted my petals caused a waterfall of pleasure to run wild inside me. He sat there and drank to his fill as he bathed me over and over again with his tongue. The steam from the hot water combined with the steam we produced left drops of dew all over me. He released me from his grip and carried me out of the sauna that was once just a bathroom.

He walked into the bedroom dripping wet holding me in his arms. He placed me at the top of his bed among the neatly placed pillows. Dade hovered over the bed while the shadows of water glistened from the street light that echoed through the window blinds. His locks were pulled back into a long ponytail. I could see the outline of his hard body and it made me want to tour the beaches of the Caribbean with him as my guide. He was rubbing oil in his hands as he climbed on top of the bed. He slowly began to coat me with the silk layer of oil. With each massage my body gave way to melodic tones. It was as if he was playing me as his own instrument. He turned me over and massaged me into him. He took my petite fleur, and caused it to bloom. He pounded his massive dick into me, causing me to let out more melodic sighs. I sang in alto soprano, hitting notes reserved for true divas. He spanked me with the force of waves crashing against the beach shoreline. I rode that wave and bucked back. Even when the sea got rough, I sailed those waters and allowed the crashes to take us ashore. I quickly took him out of me before he knew what was happening. I wrapped my lips around his massive cock and sucked all my sweet juices off him. I took all 13 inches of his industrial sized steel into my mouth. I gagged with joy as his eyes rolled back into his head. With his balls in hand I massaged and sucked. Spit and shook. I went down and up and down and up. I gently took my teeth and massaged the veins in his shaft. Up and down my mouth I went allowing him a chance to join in and sing in our duet. He pulled me off him and with force turned me around and placed the tip of his dick at the opening of my ass and with one deep breath, I exhaled and he guided himself into my cave and dominated me as only he could. I was so tight and his dick was so hard I could not stand the sensation that this pleasurable act brought. My body shook. He moaned. I tried to join the dance but the nerves of my Orpheus made me weak with emotion and drained me physically. I loved the way he carefully held me as he handled my body.

He whispered in my ear "Bae, telme yuh ok, Tell Daddee, him gyal is ok"

"Yes Daddy, your girl is ok. Daddy's girl love the way you fuck me" I sighed.

"Daddee's gyal is a good gyal, her take this dick like she own it" Dade said.

"Daddy love the way Mommy take that dick, Daddy love the way Mommy fuck that dick. "Who's dick it is Dade, tell Mommy who's dick this belong to? Who fuck you better than me Dada?" Tell Mommy who you belong to?" I sang.

Yuh, bae, Dis yuh dick gyal, Daddee only, yuh de only, yuh, Daddee dick belong to yuh onlee" he grunted out.

He took me off him and turned my lifeless body around and placed me on his lap. His dick was still hard erect. He placed me right on top of him and I rode. With him sitting off the edge of the bed I road. I road like I was on a journey. He cuffed my ass cheeks and rocked me into him. I could feel his dick inside touching the deep inner walls of my garden. He was kissing my neck. He sucked my breast. We watched each other with such intensity. He stood up with me in his arms and I road. I could feel the strength of his legs bearing down as he thrusted himself into me. His arms bulged with muscles as he held me in the air. I held on tight grabbing his moist skin. I fucked him as his dick made me sing. It was like we were at battle and no one was winning. His dick had me and my pussy, would not let him go. We repeated the pattern. With force and control we executed our dance and mastered our song. Both of us completing our quest by exploding in ecstasy.

Chapter Ten

"Foolin' Around"
– Changing Faces

"Foolin' Around"- Changing Faces

Ayanna

I woke up to a loud banging at the door. Whoever it was must have been banging at the door for a minute. Dade's phone and pager was going off. I nudged him to get up. I must have put it on him. Because his ass did not move. I could not take it anymore. I grabbed one of his shirts that was hanging on the doorknob. I closed it just enough so that if it was one of his boyz I would not flash him. I never wanted to disrespect Dade in that way. My braids flowed free as I made my way to the front door. In my haste to stop whomever was at the door from banging and waking up Dade, I did not look to see who it was. I open the door and in flew some bitch cursin' and screaming.

"Who the fuck is you" she screamed "And where the fuck is Dade"

"Look I don't know who the fuck you are but you better calm the fuck down, whatever you sellin' we don't want and whatever you looking for it aint here." I said as I was preparing to go to war. I stepped in front of her to prevent her from going any further into the house. This bitch was on one, but I aint no punk. I did not want to disrespect Dade in his shit but this bitch was about to catch a mean ass whoopin'. She steady screaming and carrying on, I had managed to drag her ass back to the door, I was getting ready to close the door on her when Dade grabbed my arm, Let go of her he said. Pushing me to the side he took her outside. And closed the door. I watched them stand there and talk. It looked like she was pleading her case and Dade was telling her off. I saw her wiping tears from her eyes. He must have told her to never show up at his house again. I felt confident that he was handling his business. Dumb bitch was no match for me. I watched as the peanut butter complexion girl stood there begging for Dade. It was pitiful. She was wearing a tank top and a pair of jeans with a pair of pink sneakers on. Her hair was pulled back in a ponytail. She looked like she came ready to fight, but even in my man's shirt that chick was no match for me. I pulled her by her ponytail and dragged her ass back to the door. I laughed as I replayed the Saturday morning drama in my head.

I walked away. Enough of this shit. I'm going to have to tell him about his bitches showing up and disrespecting me. I went back into the bedroom. Dade had me keep some cloth at his house for when I spent the night. I was going through the drawers that we shared. I found a pair of shorts and a top I could wear for the day. I pulled open the top drawer looking for a pair of panties and a matching bra. I was stopped dead in my search as I found what appeared to be a wedding band. My heart sunk just as Dade walked back in the house and closed the door behind him.

Chapter Eleven

"Come And Talk To Me"
– Jodeci

"Come and Talk to Me"-Jodeci

Yazz

Jay was not overly flashy. He drove a modest Audi. It did not have custom rims, a tricked out stereo system, or overly dark tinted glass. Even when it came to his choice of clothing, he was different from most dudes I knew. He didn't even wear a chain. Being in his line of business, he didn't want to bring unwanted attention to himself. Most niggas would brag about what they did and how much money they were making, but when it came to Jay, we knew but we didn't know. He was quiet and mostly kept to himself. He didn't even roll with the standard entourage. He was Que's right hand man and although they were mostly equals, Jay chose to play more of the background role when it came to their business. Jay was intellectual. His thoughts were deep and that's what really attracted me to him. He made love to my mind just as good as he did my body. Now don't get me wrong, his masculine honey brown frame stood all of "5'11" and commanded attention everywhere he went. He sported a 360 tapered cut and had waves for days. His eyes were a deep brown and told the story of a bitter pass, that hardened his smile and made him unapproachable to most. But with me I saw a different side of him. He was kind, soft and loving. He was the man of my dreams. I thought as we pulled up to the Elmwood Side of Delaware Park. You know the side of the park where the Museum of Arts was located and the statue of David is posted up.

Jay got out of the car, walked over to my door and opened it. He took my hand, as we walked toward the lake. I could tell that Jay had things on his mind and wanted to talk. I loved that he trusted me enough to share his inner thought and feelings. Unlike most guys I knew, the 4am hour was used exclusively for booty calls. But not Jay. When he brought me here, I knew he needed to get things off his mind. This was his escape from the world that divided us. Being here at this location gave him solace. A moment not to be in the streets, not to be on guard, not to be pained by his past. This place offered a moment to breathe. A way for Jay to be vulnerable. A way for him to be at peace. To be able to clear his mind and sleep at night. Tonight was no different. He talked and I listened. I did not say a word. I just listened. I absorbed all his pain. I gave him air and he breathed. He talked, and my soul cried, and we held each other on the park bench until the sun came up.

Chapter Twelve

"Love No Limit"
— Mary J Blige

"Love No Limit"- Mary J Blige

Yazz

I woke up to an empty bed. Jay's pager went off around 8am this morning. He kissed me on my shoulder. Jay whispered that he would be back soon. I heard the front door to his apartment close and lock behind him. I rolled over and went back to sleep. It was now 11am. I had to work today. I had a few hours before I needed to leave. I decided to get up and clean Jay's apartment. Fix something to eat and get ready for my day. I did not mind doing these things for Jay. It came second nature. I loved him and I knew he had mad love for me. He made sure that whenever I stayed at his apartment, I had everything I needed. He blessed me with a closet full of clothes, shoes and purses. I had a dresser full of all my essentials. I never had to ask. He just provided. He knew that I liked to cook, so he made sure the fridge had food and the cupboards were full. Besides eating out every day was a good way to ruin my figure and wasn't healthy, so whenever I was at his place I cooked a healthy meal for him to enjoy. I made stuffed shells and sausages. When that was done, I got ready for work. I had my standard pair of black pants and a white button down shirt on. I worked at the Jubilee grocery store located on Delaware and Great Arrow. The good thing was I worked within walking distance to Jay's apartment on Elmhurst. For days like today Jay preferred that I did not walk or take the bus. He thought too many people knew that I was with him.

"I don't want anyone to ever cause you harm because of me" he would warn. "So if I'm not here you need to take the Acura wherever you're going. This way I know you're safe." He added.

So I grabbed the keys off the key hook in the kitchen, paged Jay with the code that indicated where I was headed and out the door I went. I would see him later tonight.

I was right in the middle of my shift at work. I did not mind working. I had been working ever since I was 15 years old. I never wanted to wait for someone to hand me anything especially money, so I went and got my own. Besides working helps pay for my classes at Buff State. I was going part time, but was well on my way to earning my Bachelor's Degree in Business. I was busy ringing up a customer. I could feel the strong stares of someone watching me. I did not have time to worry about someone checking me out. It did not matter that I wasn't wearing anything sexy or tight, guys usually did not care. They knew or thought they knew me either from the club or from one of my girls. They always came into the store and tried to push up on me. So I continued cashing out my customer. When I looked up at the next person in line, there was a dude dressed in a black hoodie, black jeans with a black and white NY fitted cap on. He did not smile. He threw the pack of gum on the conveyor belt and place the bottle of Ole English down. I said hello. But he did not answer. I continued with the transaction, rung his rude ass up and stated the total.

"That will be $3:15" I announced.

He threw the money on the counter without stating a word. Rude Ass. He grabbed the bag and walked out of the store, but not before taking a look back at me. He stared as if he knew me. He stared as if I was nothing. I got chills at the thought. Weird, right?

I finished up my shift. It was now 9pm. I balanced my draw and clocked out. I still could not shake the feeling from my interchange with that guy earlier today. I was not sure what to make of it if anything. Janice and I walked out to the parking lot. I offered to take her home. She was cool, and in fact had even rolled with me and my girl to the club a few times. Without looking I went to unlock the car door using the remote car opener. I pressed the unlock key and did not hear anything. This caused me to look up and take notice and pause my conversation with Janice. There to my surprise was Jay. He had taken the Acura back to the house and came to pick me up. He greeted me with a hug and kiss. Opened our doors and chauffeured me and our guest. We dropped Janice off and headed home. The whole ride home all I kept thinking about was that customer I had. I was racking my brain trying to figure out if I knew him from somewhere, wondering if I should say something to Jay about what happened.

Back at Jay's apartment, He watched me as I got ready to go out. We had eaten dinner together and now I was putting on the finishing touches to my makeup and hair so that he could drop me off over Ayanna's. It appeared that we were gonna to be a threesome tonight as no one had heard from Anika all day. I know she was a little upset about Que, not to mention Quan's ass. But hey nothing beats the blues like new dick and money right. So I guess my girl got both for the time being. I aint mad at her. I would probably had done the same if it were me. I could not imagine my life without Jay. He has been a steady rock from me these last 10 months. I don't know why it has taken me and him so long to get together. We met about 3 years ago. I would see him with Que when they came through for Anika. I saw him looking but his shy ass never said a word. I few times I even went up to him to strike up a conversation, but it seemed as though he wasn't interested, so I kept it moving. It wasn't until he saw me coming out of Jim's Steakout on Elmwood one night that he started talking to me. I was surprised. This dude never said more than a wazzup and peace to me and here he was pressin' up on me. It was cute. So I played along. He had a girl thinking that something was wrong with me. It was not like me not to be able to pull a dude of choice. We have been together ever since.

I was finally done. I took one final look in the mirror and admired my craftsmanship. I had on a body con white strappy dress with a pair of strappy white sandals I had gotten from Baker's Shoes store. I grabbed my clutch and went to the front room to model my outfit. I could tell that Jay liked what he saw. He was chewing on a toothpick when he caught sight of the completed project. He smiled and licked his lips. He reached for my hand and pulled me into him.

He asked jokingly "You gone be alright in that tonight" holding me tight.

"You know me, a girl gotta represent" I said planting a kiss on his cheek.

"I know how you do ma. I just think it's cute, you going out getting all that attention and coming home to me. I love that you do you Yazz, I love that you bring that shit home to me"

"Damn right Pa, they can look but they can't touch" I replied with a smile.

What I really loved about Jay is he did not flip when I wanted to do me. He knew what I was about before we got together, just like I knew about him. I never got in the way of him making his money, never asked him to choose, and he did likewise. I never heard about him and any other women so I never had a reason not to bring it home and keep it there. I'm not saying I'm naive, what I'm saying is I trust him until he shows me differently. Besides I wish a bitch would try to be up on mine. It'll be the last thing she do. I got a feeling Jay would wouldn't be having that shit either.

Driving to Ayanna's, Jay's pager was going off. He had me read off the codes that came across. It made me feel like he could trust me.

"So who was that Anika was with yesterday" Jay questioned.

"Oh so you saw that" I said playin dumb.

Looking at me sideways Jay continued "You know Que gonna be pissed once I tell him right?"

I'm sure not as pissed as Anika was when he left her on the dance floor" I followed.

"True, but it's not that simple and you now that" Jay replied.

There was silence. I knew he would report that back to Que. They were boyz, hell brothers even, so keeping things from each other was a no go. And this was something I was not getting in the middle of. Anika and Que had been doing this dance for years, It wasn't my place before and it wasn't now.

All I know is a bitch aint gonna wait forever, so whatever they doing I hope they get it together soon. We arrived at Ayanna's and it appears that Monica was already there. Jay walked me to the door and as usual placed a wad of money in my hands. He smiled and kissed me and jetted back to the car as the door opened.

Chapter Thirteen

"Freaks Come Out At Night"
– Whodini

"Freaks Come out at Night"- Whodini

Yazz

We arrive at Sweetwaters Night Club located downtown Buffalo on Elm Street. It was about 10:45. The doors opened at 10 and ladies were free before 11. There was a small line. Monica knew the bouncer at the door. Teddy saw Monica and we were able to bypass the line and went straight in. We were all dressed in bodycon dresses. The atmosphere at Sweetwater's was a more mature vibe. Fellas need to dress up and ladies needed to look the part. Whenever we rolled through Sweetwaters we needed to be on point. Every baller, athlete and dude in town was present there on a Saturday Night. We always came correct, so tonight was nothing different. We found our table in the VIP. Don't ask but Monica always knew someone or did something to get us top service. On the table was a complimentary bottle of Crystal and a bottle of Hennessy. We were going to be toasting up tonight.

Ayanna

The club was packed by 11:30. We were sharing the VIP with a few DD's and athletes. The DJ was on. Me and my girls had bottles being delivered and dudes eyeing. We danced from the VIP area as people looked up at us with each move. But when they played our jams we moved to the dance floor. DJ Scratch played everything form CeCe Peniston, Jodeci, Mary J and LL. We dance to the enjoyment of all the dudes watching against the wall and for ourselves. We kept is semi classy and sexy. It was just the right amount of sass to keep the onlooker wanting more and just enough attitude to piss off the wannabe chicks that stare as if we were in the some competition.

Monica

We was living it up in VIP. My ass was flirting with the ballers and the DD's. I was tryna make moves and catch a come up. Aint nothing sadder than a bad bitch without money. If these niggas wanna trick, I'mma let 'em trick. The bottles kept coming to the table as dudes was tryna come for me and my girls. We drank, danced and drank some more. We flirted, even with the ugly dudes. Hell ugly got money too. It was all the way live. We were sexy as fuck and everyone knew it. And unlike Yazz and Ayanna I was not tryna be held down by just one nigga. I was free to flirt, fuck, dance and drink with whomever I wanted too. And tonight was no different. We showed out, and I showed my ass.

Ayanna

I was in the middle of a real nasty grind with this dude on the dance floor when from the back I felt a more authentic Jamaican twist. I turned to see who was tryna interrupt the groove, there was Dade. I turned to acknowledge him and he smiled with drink in hand. He was grinding on my butt as the song played. My arms were up in the air holding on to his locks as we rolled and twisted on the dance floor. I turned around so that he would freak me from the front. And he did. Had a girls' panties wet. He took me up to the VIP table we were sitting at. I knew what he wanted. He was nasty like that. And he knew I would not deny him. He sat back in the chair and I sat on his lap. As the people were dancing below he removed my panties and placed them in his pocket. With my dress around my waist we began to roll to the music. I moved my hips as though I was dancing and he sat there kissing on my shoulder. I moved. And with each boom of bass, the wetter my pussy became. It did not matter that people were to the right or the left of us. We grooved as if the music was playing just for us. Besides everyone was in their own world doing them. We moved in unison to the song and for a moment we were the only two people in the room. His dick was so hard. I moved and moved and moved and moved until my hips and legs gave way. He held my waist as I rolled and bounced and twisted to the song. We exploded as everyone on the floor was waving their hands in the air like they just don't care. They cheered us on and didn't even know it.

Monica

I'm yellin' where the ballers at, as I toast it up big with a couple of DD's I knew from the neighborhood. They were paid and I loved being around niggas with cheddar. They had a girl feeling rich as they popped bottle after bottle as if money was no object. I could not help but admire the gold and platinum that graced their necks, wrist and fingers. Big Mike had tried to connect with me once before, but the timing was not right, and Rich used to be with this girl I knew named Candi. I guess he and Candi went their separate ways because she normally would have her ass up here babysitting, making sure his ass wasn't fuckin around. But tonight it was all about me and how I was gonna get mine. I danced for them as if it was our own little private show. I saw them both them niggas eyein' me. Had a girl feelin' real special knowing both these niggas friends and was tryna get at me. It was a total turn on. I sat down for a minute in between Mike and Rich. Mike had his hand on my ass and Rich was on my leg. I don't think either of them knew what the other was doing but you know me, Money, Dick and Weed and not necessarily in that order. I laughed to myself as I looked at both them niggas and got up to continue dancing.

Yazz

The club was jumping and the DJ was on. Them two nasty ass bitches left me on the dance floor. It was ok. I did my thing. While I was dancing I thought for a moment that I saw the dude from earlier. He was standing in the crowd by the bar. I tried to get a better look, but by the time the guy I was dancing with moved to the right, the person was gone. It freaked me out for a moment. I kept dancing and decided to make sure I tell Jay tonight when he picks me up. After the song went off I went back up to the VIP section. I was hoping to be able to survey the room and see if I could find him again. I did not like the fact that some nigga was mean muggin me and I did not know who he was. Plus maybe one of these heifers know who this dude was and could identify him. By the time I got up to the VIP I could tell that Monica was toasted. She was livin it up with big Mike and Rich. She was crossing a very dangerous line, territory line that was. This was something I had learned from Anika. There's a few things that would scare Anika and this was one of them. DD's took pride in protecting their territory and being that we were from different hoods could only mean trouble, especially if you did not have permission. I could also smell that the too nasties had conquered the VIP section again. Ayanna and Dade were like 2 fucking bunnies. They were always humping, or worse fighting. At least for the moment all was well with those two. All I knew was I was not sitting in that chair and I had a bad feeling about that dude from earlier.

Chapter Fourteen

"I've Been Searching"
Glenn Jones

"I've Been Searching"- Glen Jones

Anika

Monday's always seems to drag. My first class was Organizational Behavior or OB. It was a required class for my Business Degree. OB is the study of human behavior in organizational settings, the interface between human behavior and the organization itself. Today we were discussing the meso level work groups. I was trying my best to stay focus, but I found myself thinking about my weekend. I must admit, I really did enjoy myself. Thinking about Mr. Cornerback brought a smile to my face. Making myself stay focused, I continued to take notes. We were assigned groups to work on our next project. I did not mind group projects. For the most part I thought the individuals in my class were mature and reliable. This was our second group assignment and if I base my opinion on the first outcome, I would say that everyone was serious about their studies. This was quite the contrary of what people thought about ECC. People in general thought ECC was for under achievers, but the truth was most of us there just could not afford higher education even with student grants. For me, I could not afford Canisius College, which is where I wanted to go and got accepted. ECC was not all bad. Granted, education is what you make of it, and for me, it was a stepping stone to something greater. There I go again drifting. Stay focus, I warned myself. By the time the professor ended the discourse I was ready to go. I touched base with my group and we decided who was to do what. We would check in with each other on Wednesday and discuss our findings before the project was due on Friday. I was out.

I hung around in the mausoleum waiting for my next class. I had about 40 minutes in between classes. I was reviewing my notes and preparing for my Macro Economics class when I was approached by a gentleman dressed in a blue suit with a white dress shirt and a blue, white and black striped tie.

"Excuse me Ms. Are you by chance, Anika Dumont?" The stranger asked.

"And who wants to know?" I replied.

"Ma'am, *was* told to tell you that your favorite Buffalo Bills player has sent a car for you and request your presence for dinner tonight, do you accept?"

I smiled and asked "why didn't he come ask me himself"

The stranger looked confused at my response. But Turned toward the stairs that lead out onto the streets of downtown Buffalo. "He said you would say that" the stranger spoke, and in walked Mr. Cornerback.

I smiled. I tried to remain cool. But I was impressed. He stood there looking hella fine. He was wearing a pair of jeans and a blue button down with the sleeves rolled up. He was wearing a fitted Buffalo Bills baseball cap. He walked over to the table where I was seated.

"I was wondering if you would like to have lunch with me?" he inquired showing his pearly whites.

"How did you find me?" I asked puzzled.

"You are a hard person to find, but I did and that's all that matters. Besides, I told you the other day I found what I've been lookin for, I'm just waiting on you" he confidently uttered.

By now a small crowd of enthusiastic Bills fans had emerged upon my table in awe of my athletic suiter. While he was busy signing autographs, I politely slipped into the background and headed to class.

Class was over and I was ready to head for home. The mausoleum was bare as I walked through it and down the stairs and out the door. To my surprise waiting outside the arched stairway, leaning against the no parking sign post was Que. His eyes were fixed on me as I exited the building. He was surrounded by a gang of groupies all wishing they could be is next victim.

"Wuz up Ma?" He said reaching for my hand as the groupies' stare with jealousy.

"What you want Que, why you here?" I asked.

"What's with the attitude Ma, I thought you would be happy to see me?" he replied with his arms open awaiting an embrace from me.

"Look Que! I'm really not interested right now. I got things to do, so don't act like you doing me any favors" I stated as I walked by him and waited for the passing cars to cross Swan Street so that I could continue walking toward the Subway.

"Hold up Anika," Que added as he began to walk with me. "Slow the fuck down" he cried as I continued to walk. He grabbed me by the arm.

I looked at him as if... and he immediately took his hand off my arm.

"Wait a minute Anika! You know I would never do anything to disrespect you, but you got me out here running after you and you know that aint my style. I came down here for you. You know I don't care about these bitches out here, yet I'm running after you. Look, you know me. You know what I'm about, you know dis. I just can't have you in this life. I can't have you upset with me. About the other day..."

I interrupted him "Look Que, you don't owe me anything. I got it. You don't want me and I'm ok with that. What I'm not ok with is you showing up here acting like you care. We friends that's all nothing else. So you can stop running after me, cause I'm not running toward you. We good. I gotta go," I said as I continued to walk away. This time my pace was even faster. I did not look back, because I knew in my heart he wouldn't chase after me. And I would never be number one in his life.

Waiting at the Utica Station I began to think about Me and Que. Our history. The story of us. I will never forget that day. My family is a two parter. There's the good side and the bad side. My mother never allowed us to really associate with my family in the Fruit Belt. They dabbled in what was known as the family business. Now my grandfather and grandmother took us over there on a regular basis. So I got to know my cousins really well. It did not matter to me at the time what our family did, family was family. But as we became teenagers, the dynamics of the family business were changing. The Fruit Belt became known as a notorious drug neighborhood. You didn't hang out in the "Belt" unless you were looking for trouble. My cousins were starting to take hold of the family business and were slowly expanding the business in other wards of the city. We were powerful and everyone feared the name. My cousin Moe and Rob were now in charge. They had made it very clear to me and a few other female cousins how unsafe it would be for us to date any dudes from warring neighborhoods. All my male cousins were aware and pretty much knew the laws of the street, but the female cousins were often vulnerable and targeted by rival drug families. So, to be safe, we were never allowed to date outside the family domain, let alone be in certain areas of town without permission. But my fast-ass let that sermon go right in one ear and out the other.

I was attending a party in the Doat area of town. Now normally this was a no no,

but I never missed an opportunity to party and show off my assets. Plus there would be new niggas. I was so tired of seeing the same ole dudes. So we went. Me, Monica, and Yazz. We were having a blast. Dudes were checking for us and girls were hating. Other than the usual stares and glares, no significant issues popped off. The DJ started to slow the music down and I was approached by this guy name Bam. Bam was a local DD. Everyone knew who he was. He drove a candy apple red Mustang 5.0 and a Red and white custom colored Bronco with the darkest tints I've ever seen. The outside of the windows were glazed like mirrors. He asked me to dance. "Slow Dance" by R. Kelly was playin through the speakers. He took me by the waist and held me close. I was flattered. I could tell all the neighborhood chicks were staring at me with him. We danced slow and grinded hard with every turn we took. He cuffed my ass and I liked it. We danced and he sang the song in my ear. It was cute. He could not carry a tune to save his life, but it did not matter. After that night he was a constant figure in my world.

We were dating for about 6 months. I kept our relationship a secret. One, my parents would disagree with my choices and second I was breaking a huge rule. One I would soon regret breaking. I had introduced my girls to his boyz. We rode around town in a rainbow of colored 5.0's. We got all kinds of dirty looks from girls as we showed up with Bam and his crew. They balled out on us and we loved it. One day Bam was tied up doing business and I was with him. I wanted to go to the mall. He told me to take his truck. He gave me a stack of money and told me to have fun. I took this time to floss. I drove around showing off. I had the music blastin' and the windows was slightly rolled down, just enough to allow the wind to run through the truck. I was stopped by the light at the corner of Sycamore and Fillmore. There was a car behind me with two guys in it. I paid them little attention. The light turned green. We proceeded to the intersection at Fillmore and Genesee. The light turned red. Before I knew what happened, the truck door opened, and there stood 2 armed, masked niggas. They looked confused as if they were expecting someone else. It was broad daylight and I thought it was my last. Pointing their guns in my face I was given a stern message.

"Tell that punk muthafucka Bam we said next time it will be him."

"Bang, Bang Bitch!" the same masked gunman yelled.

The first gunman kept looking at me. His eyes familiar. He grabbed me out of the truck only after taking the keys out the ignition and turning the truck off.

I was in tears not to mention scared. I peed my skirt. Damn near shitted on myself at the thought of what they were going to do to me. He threw me in the back seat of the car they were in and drove off. I was too frightened to ask any questions. I tried, but could not regain my composure.

"Shut the fuck up" the familiar eyed masked man said.

We quickly pulled off onto a sparsely occupied street. The 2 gunmen were arguing. They both stepped out of the car. All I could do was cry. My cries drowned out anything they were saying. One guy got back in the car. We sped off. Not knowing what to do, I prayed. I thought about my family, my girls, I even thought about Bam. The tears continued to roll down my face. I cried. I cried because I knew better.

We drove. I didn't even notice that the gunman had removed his mask.

"Calm the fuck down Anika" The voice yelled.

Did he just say my name? I could not understand. My eyes were swollen from crying. Who, what umm? I was confused as the voice continued to speak.

"Stop crying, wipe your eyes and listen" the voice commanded.

He had my full attention.

"What the fuck were you doing driving that niggas truck huh? Do you know what could have just happened back there? Do you know the predicament you put me in? Yourself? What the fuck were you thinking?" he yelled questioning.

I dare not answer as I'm sure he did not want to hear my responses. We pulled up to a house, rolled into the driveway and in the garage. The garage door closed behind us. My door opened and he grabbed me and rushed me into the house. He shoved me into the chair located in the living room. He walked away and went into the bathroom, I heard him turn the water on. He came back handed me a towel and washcloth and told me to go get cleaned up. I was hesitant, but the thought of him asking me again to do something scared me even more. I walked with a purpose to the bathroom still barely able to see. He had started the shower. I took off the wet clothes that now echoed the smell of fresh pee. There was a bag on the counter for me to place my items in. I stepped into the shower. I tried to wash my current situation away. I cried and tried to get it together. But the thought that I was in serious danger hung over me. I cried. There was a knock on the door and the voice told me to hurry up. I turned the water off and quickly dried off. Wrapped in my towel I noticed the voice had thrown some jeans and a tank on the floor for me to wear. I got dressed and hesitantly opened the door.

Que. My eyes were deflated enough to identify him. I could hear him on the phone explaining the events of the day to whom I could assume was either Maurice or Rob. I knew I was in trouble. Que noticed that I was out of the bathroom and he ended the conversation. He stared at me angrily.

"I can explain" I pleaded.

"Explain what Anika? That I almost killed you or why you were driving that bitch ass niggaz' car?"

"What?" he screamed.

"Do you know how much trouble you're in? How much trouble you've caused? Now I have to clean this shit up. This is fucked up Ma. Fucked up!" he said pacing back and forth.

I just sat there in the chair. My heart sank and I could feel the tears choking their way back up my throat.

"You better not" he said. "We are beyond crying now. You should have thought about that before you went off and did your own thing".

The number 13 Kensington bus rode up and broke my thoughts of the events that bind Que and I together. There was a small group of us lined up to board. I flashed the bus drive my metro pass and boarded the bus. I sat in the second set of forward facing seats. I continued to think about that day and the events that happened as a result of my actions. The bus drove off. As I continued my thoughts and flashed back in time. I confessed my actions to Que and he to Maurice and Rob. I took a tongue lashing and the consequences that followed. Until they could make sure I was not in immediate danger, I had to stay with Que. He was assigned to babysit me over the next few days. At first it was an interrogation fest, as I was grilled about Bam and his crew. I had to give up details and the who and what of every question they asked. I also had to make sure my girls were ok. So they too were placed on lockdown. My bodyguard was rude and inhospitable. But under the circumstances I kept the attitude to a minimum. Que kept it very professional. He would not really speak with me and at times seemed to only be in the same room with me for short periods of time. I was becoming bored with my surroundings. I really wanted to go outside and breathe. I had not been out of the house since my arrival. Plus the constant look of disapproval from Que was killing me. While he was on the phone one afternoon, I decided to take a walk and head to the store.

Before I could get 10 steps down the street a car pulls up with soldiers who were guarding the house and Que storms out the door just as quick. That's when I began to see how real this situation was.

Days turned into weeks. My parents thought I was spending time at Ayanna's out in Tonawanda. It was summertime and this would be acceptable behavior on my part. But my reality was nothing but. I had overheard Que talking about how they needed to contain the situation. That war was going to happen. I was scared. But whenever I would enter the room he would end the calls.

One night while eating dinner, Que seemed relaxed enough and I had mustered up enough courage to ask him what was happening. I was not ready to hear what he divulged to me. We were headed to war. After the situation with Bam and the truck, word on the street was that he thought I had been taken. However, he quickly learned that I was family to the Fruit Belt, so it seemed as if I was setting him up. He and his crew have been looking for me, which is why I had to stay with Que. My cousins trusted Que like he was family. They knew he would not allow anything to happen to me. Que continued to tell me that Bam had to go. He and his crew were now a threat. War was imminent for the family to expand, but because of my fucked situation, the schedule has been accelerated.

At the end of week 2 things seemed to be quiet. Que had gone grocery and clothes shopping for me. He picked up some essentials for me as it looked like I was not going home anytime soon. He made sure I checked in with my Parents and that I spoke with my girls to make sure that they were ok and if they had heard anything about me or Bam. Monica said that they did approach her and ask if she saw me. She told them she hadn't seen me in weeks, which was true. She stated that Bam's car rolls down the street almost every day like he lookin for me. Other than that no one had anything to report. All my girls knew was that I was not to be seen and if anyone ask I was with Ayanna -who was in North Carolina visiting family for the next month. I did call her to let her know that she was my cover just in case someone asked.

It was about 10:30pm. I was locked in the house. Que had an errand to run and there was a parked car out front keeping watch. I would occasionally peek out the window to see what was going on. I took a peek and noticed that the car with the 2 unnamed guards was not posted up out front. I thought it was weird, but not really as they were not allowed in the house. They have been known to ride up and down the block, or even go to pick up food or take a bathroom break. But when Que went out, which was rare, they were to stay put. I distinctly recall him telling them not too fuckin blink or take their eyes off the house. I was sure they would return before Que noticed that they did not hold their ground. The phone rang. This was rare. I haven't heard the phone ring since my arrival. I ignored it, but it kept ringing. I finally answered. There was no one there. It rang again. I answered, but there was no one on the other end. About 30 min went by and the house was quiet. I peeked outside the window again and no car. No sign of any guards. Where was Que.

I fell asleep. I woke up to the sounds of the TV and the infomercial that was playing. It was 1am. I could tell that Que was not home. I walked into the kitchen to get a drink of water.

"Ouch" I screamed. I had walked on something sharp and cut my foot. I manage to make my way back to the bathroom. I cleaned up my foot and hobbled my way back into the front, but not before I was greeted by a familiar voice coming from the living room.

"So dis where you been hiding bitch! Had a nigga worried about you and shit. But naw your ass just up and left my shit at the corner like fuck it!" Bam yelled.

I was scared "Bam baby, I can.."

"You can what? Tell me who the fuck you are? Explain to me how you planned to set me up"? he yelled as he rose off the couch and started towards me.

I screamed! I ran and headed toward the bedroom. I tried locking the door, but Bam kicked the door in. I was pleading for my life as he grabbed and punched me.

"You dumb bitch! You gonna set me up? You think I'm stupid, that I don't know who you are?" he yelled spitting as he talked.

No Bam don't, I wouldn't do that, it shouldn't matter who I am, you know me!" I managed to get out as he placed his hands around my neck.

We were wrestling on the bed but his 220lb frame was too much for me. He grabbed me by my hair and held me down as she started ripping my clothes off.

"Don't" I begged. I pleaded. Up until this point I was a virgin. Everyone assumed that I was having sex, but truth be told, I was just a tease. I remembered what my daddy said about girls who gave away their cookie. And how guys used girls like me. That holding onto my prize was the one gift I could give my husband or someone special. I could see my father's face as I fought for my life. I could see him guiding me through this fight. I could hear his voice sayin "don't let this nigga get the best of you." I fought with all the force of my 4 brothers. But Bam hovered over me like a dead sack of potatoes. I bit and scratched, I screamed and hit, I cried out for Que! I had cried out for the lost little girl I was in this moment and for the women I wanted to become. Bam had beat me almost into submission. I had been slapped and punched all over my body. I could taste my virgin blood as it dripped down my throat. I fought and cried. And as he was about to take me, I heard the loud bang of a gun, saw the bright streak of light and felt warm liquid seeping onto me. I screamed for Que! And I gasped for air as the room went dark.

We approached my stop. I pulled the string to ring for the bus driver to stop at the next bus stop. I exited the bus at the corner of Humboldt and E. Ferry. I was shaken reliving the moments that lead up to that night. Just thinking about it makes my soul hurt. The light changed red and I proceeded to cross the street. I was so unfocused and not aware of my surroundings as I was stuck in that moment. I did not hear my neighbors speak to me nor hear the car load of hotties try to get at me. I went back to my thoughts.

All I remember was Que picking my battered body up and escorting me out of the room.

"You're ok now, I got you, I'll never let anything happen to you, baby" He kissed me repeatedly.

I shook with fear, I wanted to go. I wanted him to take me away. I blacked out. I woke to find myself in Que's arms. He held me tight. I was covered in a blanket. We lay on the bed except we were not in the same house. The sun was shining through the windows and I could hear the birds singing outside. I moved and he woke up. He looked at me and kissed my cheeks and forehead. My body ached. My face felt punished. I began to cry as I thought about the events of last night. He held me and whispered "Everything is ok, he will never hurt you again. I will not allow anything to happen to you again. I'll always protect you." He whispered over and over until I fell back to sleep in his arms.

I made it home. I was the only person home for the time being. I threw my belongings into my bedroom and went back onto the porch and sat in the hot summer sun as the hustle and bustle of a busy city street took me back to my thoughts. I'm not sure how many days I had been out. But when I can to, Monica and Yazz were by my side. Que walked in with some broth and crackers. He said I needed to eat. It appeared as though they had been waiting for me to come to for a while. I tried to sit up but my head hurt bad. With every breath I took, my sides hurt and tears began to swell up in my eyes. Que who was sitting by my side, would kiss my tears away. I could barely talk. He told me that he would be just outside the room if I needed him. He was going to let Monica and Yazz take care of me. I sat there wrapped like a mummy as Bam must have cracked my ribs. Monica propped a pillow behind me so that I could sit up comfortably.

As soon as Que existed the room, they could not wait to tell me everything they knew. Monica went first as she said with excitement.

"Girl Que shot that nigga!!"

"We don't know that" said Yazz. "What we do know is that they found Bam's body in an abandoned house. They found him and three of the dudes we rode with. Their mustangs were set on fire in various hoods throughout the east side. There was also a big drug bust on Doat. They picked up Bam's entire crew. It was all over the news." finished Yazz.

"Girl that nigga been right here by your side" Monica proclaimed as she was trying to feed me broth.

"Girl Que came and got us the day after it all went down. Made us promise not to tell a soul where you were. Said he needed our help." added Yazz.

"I see how he look at you, that nigga love you" Monica chimed in.

I sat there absorbing everything they were saying. Was it possible? Que killed Bam. I was there but I could not collaborate their story. Did he kill Bam, did he save me? Thinking of the event brought tears to my eyes. As much as I was happy to see Monica and Yazz, I wanted to be by myself. Que returned to the room and could tell I was overwhelmed. He told the girls that was enough excitement for today. They could come back tomorrow to visit. They looked back at him, winked at me and said they would be back tomorrow with ice cream.

"Crazy Vanilla right?" Monica yelled to confirm. I smiled even though it hurt.

Over the next couple of days Que nursed me back to health. I think in a way I nursed him back to. He was gentle with me. Not like the Que I had come to know. We went from him pulling my ponytails on the playground whenever I visited my cousins in the Fruit Belt, to not speaking to me at all. And here we were. We talked, we laughed, I cried and he was there to wipe my tears away. Que was 4 years older than me. But in this moment, I knew age did not matter. I could tell he was catching feelings as was I. One night I took my shower and he helped me get out of the bath. He helped me dry off. He tried not to look. But my body was too enticing. He looked as I stood there naked with my wounded body. I craved his touch. He kissed me and ran his hand down the side of my body. I wanted him. My savior, my hero. I needed him to end this pain to stop my nightmare. I needed him to allow me to present my gift to him, untampered and pure. I wanted him to take the cookie and leave no crumbs.

He carried me to the bedroom and began kissing my bruises. He kissed me gently. His touch was soft as he caressed my breast and worked down my body. How different his touch was in this moment than the last man who wanted me. What a contrast. My being naked and wanting verses my being naked and afraid. I needed him to love me. I had been searching and waiting. Que. He licked and kissed his way to my cookie. Looking up at me our eyes locked and he devoured me like it was his first and he was my first. He held my body in his hands, as he drank from my soul. I presented a perfect gift offering and he accepted. My temple had not been defiled and he worshipped me with every moment of his tongue. I moaned a chorus of hymns and the heavens approved as the man opened my temple up to be adorned. He entered me with the force of a million horses and the power of lightning. His power was thick and long, hard and swollen. My alter had never imagined this moment quite like this. The pleasurable pain that overcame me wiped my fears away. He loved me with such tenderness and care. He penetrated my inner sanctuary, humbling himself to me. I gave way to angelic sounds of praise as he presented thrusting gifts of myr and oils and fine gold. I held his body tight as to welcome him not only by my lips but through my lips. I sang and he showered in my gifts. I returned his thrust with showers of pure heavenly waters. I gave and he received. He gave and I received. Our bodies in unison resembling a beautiful painting. I had given him the key to my temple and he had entered and entered and entered. He had claimed what no man could and for that we will always have this moment. We had crossed a line. My protector was doing his job and I allowed him to serve me, protect me to the fullest.

I sat there in Que arms having a sense of calm. He kissed my forehead. He held me tight. With no words we knew. I wanted to pretend that he could always be here in this moment with me. That he would be mines and only mines by I knew in my heart, he belonged to the streets. He belonged to my family and that I could never win.

Chapter Fifteen

"Aint Too Proud To Beg"
– TLC

"Aint 2 Proud 2 Beg"-TLC

Ayanna-

Just because we had a good time in the club, don't mean I aint pissed. So that Jamaican nigga playing games? I got him. He can't control his bitches, now they coming to the house. And what the fuck was that ring shit about? I'll show him he can either get his shit together or I'll get it together for him. You know what? I'll show him how this shit feels. He wanna play games, keep secrets, I'll show him. I thought as I left the house. I was wearing a pink tank top with a pair of white daisy duke shorts and a pair of pink esprillias. I hopped in the jeep wrangler that was parked in the garage. It was a hot summer day. I just heard on the radio weather report that today's high would reach 90 degrees. I was ready. All I needed now was a partner in crime and I'm sure we could find some trouble to get into. I went to pick up Monica and we headed up to Delaware park to catch the ball players in action. Monica was wearing a tight short mini skirt with a tank top. She had on a strappy pair of flat sandals. We were looking cute. When we rolled out it was like magic. Everyone stopped to stare. We were hood stars and we loved it. With beats blasting and the bass thumping we headed to the park to see what kind of trouble we could get into. Before entering the park, we stopped at the store. We both got out of the car.

"Damn Mamma"

"Hey cutie"

Someone even whistled at us, It was cute. I knew that my outfit was fly. Hell you would be hard pressed to catch me and my girls ever looking raggedy. Anytime we hit the streets we were representing. We were fine. Dudes always were tryna get with us. They also knew what it would take to pull a girl like us. So cat calls did not warrant my time. It was flattering, but Mammie need more than just a nigga hanging on the corner, he needed to own the corner. But It was good to know that the outfits were on point. We walked into the store. I purchased 2 blow pops, 2 popsicles and a water. Monica got a Philly, water, 2 freezes and a blow pop. We jumped back into the jeep and headed for the park.

Monica

I don't know what the fuck happened between Ayanna and Dade, but I knew that look in Ayanna's eyes and we were getting ready to start some shit. We arrived at

Delaware Park and the basketball court was packed. There were hotties err'where. We drove through to take a look at who was all out there. I had to admit, I loved riding in the Wrangler with the top and doors off. This gave niggas a better look at what was inside, besides the wind blowing through my hair was a welcome treat on a day like today. I was able to get my tan and mack on at the same time. We were making our second lap through when we found a good parking spot. We pulled over just shy of the basketball court. I walked over to the court and stood on the sideline. There was dudes galore! I'm talkin' buffet! There was a little of everything that could please a girl with an appetite like mines. There were short stocky dudes, tall thin, broad shoulders, juice asses, muscles, calves, arms, bald heads, waves, brown eyes, hazel, dark, light and everything in between. The fellas were out he flexin' and I was ready to be served. I was plotting how to stack my plate as I stood there catching stares. I stood there sucking on my freeze. It was hot and I could not think of a better way to cool off and show off some skillz. I deep throated that baby and sucked the flavor out of it until the ice was white again. I stood there cheering for my eye candy as I bounced with joy as they made baskets and blocks and ran up and down the court trying to impress the chicks that were all competing for attention. Me, no competition. I was a one of a kind. I "accidentally" dropped my keys and with the skillz of a striper in church, seductively bent down to pick up my keys and brung it back up with my ass facing the court. All I knew was that I did not hear single word, not even the ball bounced. I turned around and smiled as dudes were hi fiving each other and commenting on my well developed assets. I stuck my almost bare leg out to the side and stood with attitude. The game was about to end and I heard others calling for next.

One player walked over to me and asked, "If I make this next shot, you gone give me a sip of your water?" dribbling the ball holding up the game.

I laughed and said "Sure, but you gotta dunk it if you want more than a sip." Flirting with me he smiled and said "ok."

He dribbled the ball, passed it to one guy, motioned for the ball back and with one smooth bounce, he headed toward the basket, looked back at me and with both hands on the ball, became airborne and jammed the ball in the hoop. The crowd went wild and my pussy became wet.

The game was over and he walked over to me. He was tall, with a peanut butter complexion, dimples, medium build with tight muscular arms. He wore a diamond stud the size of a raisin in his right ear. He was wearing a pair of white mesh b-ball shorts with a Syracuse sleeveless tee. He was sweaty and the beads of sweat sparkled as the sun hit him. He removed his tee shirt to wipe the sweat off of him.

"What about my sip of water" he inquired staring at me with his deep brown eyes.

I handed him my water. He took 2 sips and added "So what do I get for dunkin' that ball for you?" smiling bashfully.

I took my hand and ran it across is well defined abs, "You can have whatever you want, but for now let me cool you off" I said. And without thinking I poured my water all over his head and chest. He was shocked, but enjoyed the cool water. I laughed and he smiled as I backed away from him as he reached for me. He was soaking wet and sweaty.

"I'mma make you pay for that" he growled.

I laughed, and threw the bottle of water at him as he began to chase after me. He caught me and picked me up from behind. He was carrying me back toward the court.

"You smell as good as you look" he whispered. "Today must be my lucky day, you show up, I dunked and won the game. You might be my lucky charm" he continued.

"Put me down" I flirtatiously uttered trying but not trying to get out of his grasp.

We made our way back to his car. He opened the door and pulled out a towel. I grabbed it from him and began to wipe the sweat off his body. I wiped his head, down his chest to his belly button. It was an outie. I told him to turn around as I proceeded to dry off his back. I asked, "Is there anything else that needs drying off" I said smiling and tugging at his gym shorts.

"Wow shorty, you bold as hell. You always like this?" He asked. "I like your style" he continued.

"I like what I see too" I commented. I'm hoping I'd like what's in those shorts I thought to myself.

We talked for a moment and exchanged numbers.

"This isn't a fake number is it he asked, it would break my heart if we don't hook up later" Shawn added.

Yeah Shawn was his name. "Now do I look like the type that would give out a fake number", I said jokingly

"Yeah you do! In fact you look like the type that might have a badass boyfriend that would kill me for fucking with you" he replied.

"Not me. I'm as real as they come, trust and believe me on that. But for real, Hit me up later and we can get together" I assured him.

"Cool Monica" he said as I walked away back over to the basketball court. I looked back to notice him watching my ass shake as I walked through the uneven grass in my espadrilles.

Ayanna

I was sucking on my popsicle. The heat was melting it fast. It was blue raspberry flavored. I tried to keep up with the drips of blue colored water that cascaded down the popsicle. I licked, and licked. I rode my month up the sides of the popsicle. I swallowed the whole popsicle. I took it deep and allowed it to quench my thirst. My lips closing at the point that the iced flavored water meets the wooden stick. I tilted my head back to allow the juice to run down my throat. I sucked and sucked and without knowing had managed to attract many suitors with my popsicle eating skills. I smiled as I was finally conquered sucking the popsicle and there were no traces of it as I brought forth the wooden sticks that once held a flavorful ice block that turned my tongue blue.

"Damn Ma! I'll run to the store right now and buy 4 more popsicles if I can see you do it again" one dude yelled.

"That shit was impressive!" another said.

"Can I be your next popsicle?" a tall chocolate dude said.

"That depends, what flavor are you" I replied

"Chocolate. So I hope you like fudge" he confidently continued.

"I love chocolate and fudgesicles" I said smiling as he approached me.

"Is that so" he smiled showing off his perfectly white teeth.

"If you didn't notice I love popsicles, especially on hot days like today." I said leaning into my stance, which now had me with my breast and ass slightly protruding.

"Hey Sam, you gonna play or what?" one of his homies yelled as the next game was getting ready to start.

"Go ahead Sam, I'll be here when you're done. Then we can see about me and your fudgesicle" I encouraged as his eyes widen at the thought.

"Bet" he said.

Don't know if Sam was showing off for me or if he really had mad skillz. The boy could ball. I heard that he played overseas for Spain. Either way. I was watching with excitement as he ran up and down the court. I watched the way his body moved. He was shirtless so his abs were banging. He had broad shoulders and very muscular legs. All I could imagine was my legs wrapped around that body. I'm not sure if dudes wear jock straps when playing basketball, but Sam's dick was swinging. It appeared to be long and solid. I could see his imprint through his silky black gym shorts. And all I wanted was a fudgesicle. Really bad.

Monica was at the jeep talking to some dudes. She turned on the car and let the music play. I had reggae playing. It was a mega mix tape. Mad Cobra was playing. All the girls at the court started dancing as Cobra began singing "Flex time to have sex, Longtime yuh have di rude bwoy yah a sweet girl, flex time to have sex".

Our bodies began to roll. It was a distraction to the ball players. I was no different. My body whined and my hips rolled as if I was at the club. A few dudes on the court stopped and started boggling. It was funny. I was dancing by 2 dudes who stood up and joined me in my slow whine. It was a party. Monica was rolling her ass on some dude as he posted up on the jeep. The other dude enjoyed her from the front. I had the exclusive cut of Bennie Man Who am I Sim Simma, almost 2 years before it hit the US. It was hot. It blasted through the Jeep next and the crowd at the courts went wild. We continued to dance. Reggae style.

"Uhhh na na na na oh na naa oh na na eh,

Sim simma, who got the keys to ma bimma,

Who am I, de girls dem suga

How can I mek luv to a fema in ah rush

Pass me da keys to my truck

Who am I, de girls dem look

And I and I will make luv to precious"

we all sang along. It was the unofficial halftime show.

I stepped on the court like it was a dance floor and showed out. I went all out Jamaican. I whined and rolled and ticked like I was born in the islands. The crowd went wild and one guy stepped up and joined in. We whined and I ticked my ass all over him in my booty shorts. I did the handstand and freaked him hard real quick to the cheers of the dudes and became the instant role model of all the girls who hadn't mastered their skills. Life goal, be like me.

We finished the mixtape with Shabba Ranks "Trailer Load of Girls". By this time, Monica had made her way over to the basketball court and she joined me in dance. We broke it down. And people driving by stopped to see the show. It was the perfect way to end the afternoon. I did not care who saw me. I was out for self and not once did I think of Dade finding out. Sam joined me in a tick off as I rub a dubbed all over him and his sweaty ass. I might as well had fucked him. His dick was so hard. I went down on my hands and ticked and whined it up and went as far back as I could extend and worked him. I could tell he was impressed. I was impressed too, he could hang. I was definitely interested in seeing that fudgesicle after that.

We ended our adventure at the park as planned. We caused some commotion, made some friends, and then left. We came. We saw. We conquered. I left with Sam's number. He promised to hit me up later tonight. By them, I'll be more than ready to cool off with that fudgesicle.

Chapter Sixteen

"You Can Call Me Crazy"
– Guy

"You Can Call me Crazy" - Guy

Yazz

Jay dropped me off at my place last night he had business to take care. He planned on stopping back by when he was done. He had a key to my place so I was ok with him coming and going at all hours of the day. Jay had an alarm system installed a while back just in case. That nigga was paranoid on the low. I woke up to find Jay sound asleep next to me. I did not want to wake him but I really wanted to get in a quick run before the day started. It was about 6:30 am when I left the house. The only people up at this time were third shifters heading home or night owls that partied the night away. I loved the summer time. The sun seemed to greet me and give me the much need energy to stay on my grind. There were 2 things I could not stand and one being women who get a man and let themselves go. I mean you do all that to catch them, dress sexy, makeup be on point, suck the hell out of that dick, fuck them on a regular, not to mention hair and nails did. Then turn around and get lazy and act like they men gonna stand for that. That's why it's been so easy for me and my girls to get a M&M (Married Man). We used to pull them like candy when we went out. If their wives wouldn't do it we would. And they loved that shit. They would do whatever we asked and in return we would fuck the shit out of them. We had niggas wanting to leave their wives for the pussy. It was crazy. That shit will not happen to me. I will keep my body tight. I will always stay true to the code. Fuck and Suck. You have to do what you did to get him and you do what you did to keep'em. So I made sure that kept myself fly as hell and my body tight, just like he found me. So if I can only find time to run early mornings then I run early mornings.

I quietly got dressed. I was wearing a pair of biker shorts and a sports bra. I headed out for my daily run. I had mapped out my 3mile run. I either did a 3 or 5 mile run and since I was at home and not close to Delaware park I decided to just run the 3 miles today. That way I could get home and washed up before Jay wakes up. I headed out the door. Stretched and began my journey around my hood. My braids were pulled up in a ponytail. I ran down Eggert, turned at Kensington headed toward Harlem Rd. I ran at a good pace. Pass the Wilson Farms. I made it too Kenview Blvd when I noticed a car. A dark blue Bronco. I had seen the same car pass me about 3 streets back on Eggert.

The same dark blue Bronco had now pass me 3 times in both directions. The driver was a female. She would stare as she rode past me. I'm now zoned in. I knew it was not a coincidence. I'm sure that someone is following me, but why? It was not time for me to panic, besides I'm hood, aint nobody gonna come for me without a fight. I turned around and headed back home. Instead of my usual route, I decided to cut the run short. I turned around and headed back cutting down Century Rd to Cleveland Dr. and through Kensington Village. By the time the car caught up to me it was too late, I had lost them.

I entered the house out of breath. I set the alarm and went to wake Jay. But when I got to the bedroom Jay was gone. Damn it Jay! I paged him 911 with my code. He knew I would not use the 911 unless it was a true emergency. I don't know what the fuck is going on but I'm sure as hell not going to sit here and wait. I began packing some clothes. I would give Jay 15mins to call back. If he did not call me back by then, I would head to his place and wait, better yet I would go to Anika's. I grabbed the gun, Jay had given me. He taught me how to shoot it. He had given me lessons a while ago when we first started dating. I never thought I was going to have to use it. Whoever was fucking with me didn't know I would be ready. Where are you Jay I screamed! I could not wait any longer. I will page him when I get to Anika's. I headed out the door, jumped into my car and pulled off.

I made sure no one was following me as I was driving. I made sure that I checked every car that got behind or on the side of me. Every face became an enemy. I started thinking of the car that was following me. I was trying to recall the face of the girl that was following me. I could not place her. I was thinking about the guy from the other day. I was wondering if the 2 were connected. All I know was Jay would know what to do. I needed to find him. I needed to tell him what the fuck was going on. I pulled up to Anika's house. I rang the doorbell. The screen door was locked. Anika came to the door.

"Damn girl, what's the rush?" Anika questioned.

"Girl let me in" I demanded and locked the screen door as I entered her home. I was shaking. She could tell something was wrong.

"What's up Yazz? You're scaring me" Anika asked.

"I need to use the phone, I need to page Jay." I stated as I took hold of the phone and sat down on the couch. I paged Jay 911 and my code. Within 3 minutes the phone rang.

Anika answered.

"Hello" Anika sang.

"Jay, something is wrong with Yazz, she's scaring me here talk to her" she finished handing me the phone.

"Jay, I need you to come right now, we need to talk, now. I'll tell you when you get here." I hung up the phone. Jay said that he would be here in 10 minutes. I filled Anika in on what has been happening. About the dude at the store and again at the club. I told her about the girl in the dark blue Bronco. I asked her if she thought I was crazy. She said "Naw, you have to trust your gut". She thought I should have told him about the dude at the store right after it happened.

"You can never be too careful, you know Jay and Que be into some shit, you never know who tryna get at them through us" she stated as she hugged me.

Just then the doorbell rang I could see through the screen that it was Jay and Que. I told them about the dude at the store and what happened at the club then this morning. Jay grew more and more upset as I relived the encounters. He and Que just looked at each other. I knew they knew what this was all about. Que asked if Anika's mom was home, she told him she had left for work and that she was the only one here.

"Good, you two will ok here until we get back" Que stated.

"What do you mean safe, what is this about?" I demanded to know.

"Wait Que, what is this about?" Anika questioned.

"We will explain everything to you later" Jay added. "For now, just sit tight and will be back in an hour tops".

Que and Jay left and we locked the door behind them. Both of us not sure what to make of this, but we knew that shit was about to go down. We just hoped nobody we knew were in the crossfire.

Chapter Seventeen

"Looking At The Front Door"
– Main Source

"Looking At The Front Door"-Main Source

Ayanna

After dropping Monica off at her house I went home to relax. Needed to wash the sweaty afternoon off of me. I went upstairs to the bathroom. I ran the water for the shower and immediately undressed and enjoyed my cleansing. My shower quickly turned sour as I heard the door open and in walked Dade. He had crawled from whatever rock he was under and decided to bless me with his presence. He was butt ass naked and interrupting my shower. He did not ask he just did. So there I was with the source of my anger. I can't lie my body wanted him, but I was going to stay true to my heart for once. Maybe it was time that he and I go our separate ways. Maybe I should just be ok with our arrangement. Maybe I should just be happy, knowing that I have someone. Bitch maybe you deserve better. Maybe you need more that he can give, I thought as the hot water hit my body. Enough. Dade started to touch my body. Ooh how I loved his touch. Girl get your ass out of this shower before you regret it, I had warned myself silently. If he wanted you he was going to have to prove it or at least explain that damn wedding band I found in my drawer. I quickly excused myself from the shower and walked away.

I was drying off when my phone rang. I grabbed the cordless and answered. It was the hottie from the park. Sam's voice sounded good. It was seductive, strong and welcoming. I carried on the conversation as if I was home alone without a care in the world. I sat on the bed in my panties and bra lotioning my body, making plans for him to pick me up. Now this would be a first. Me having a guy stop by the house was a NO NO! I was not willing to take the chance that Dade would show up or even find out. He had way too many people looking out for him. It was bad enough I did my dirty on the side, but to have a name or even face to go with it was like putting the bullet in the gun. Dade was crazy, and that might just have that nigga on edge. But fuck him. Maybe he needs to be on edge. Maybe he needs to see me with someone else. Maybe then he will come to his senses and appreciate me.

"Tonight at 8 sounds good to me" I said smiling and hung up the phone just as Dade walked in the room.

"Tonight at 8 what?" he asked smacking me on my ass.

"I'm going out" I replied. "I'm getting the fuck out!!"

Chapter Eighteen

"Is It Good To You"
– Heavy D and the Boyz

"Is It Good To you" Heavy D and the Boyz

Anika

I can only imagine what Yazz is going through. Not too long ago I was in that same space. Just as promised, Jay was back within the hour to pick Yazz up. I looked for a shadow to follow him in the door but to my surprise Que was absent from this visit.

Jay escorted Yazz to the car. I kissed her and told her not to worry as she was in good hands. If Jay was anything like Que he would not allow anything to happen to her. Plus they got mad love for each other and in my mind sometimes that's all you need to conquer the bad.

"Hey Anika, Que said he would hit you up in about an hour" Jay said opening the door for Yazz.

"Ok, Jay. Take good care of her I said", wanting to go with her to make sure she would be ok. But I knew that as hard as it is to protect one person, adding another to the mix would just complicate things. Besides, I don't know what the fuck the problem is and if there is a solution. I'm tired of going into things blind. And this felt like some shit and fuckery that none of us were prepared for.

I was finishing up my portion of the Group homework assignment for my OB Class. I had just received the last bit of information from Sara, who was in my group. I had typed the final paragraph when there was a knock at the door. After Yazz left, I thought it was best If I closed door and locked the door. I did not want to take any unnecessary chances. Mr. Cornerback was standing at the door facing the now busy street. I opened the door. He was dressed in a navy blue suit that was tailor made for his body. With a crisp white button down shirt, an orange, blue and white paisley print bow tie, with an abstract pocket square. He wore a nice Italian pair of leather brown wingtip shoes that were polished to shine. Damn he was a welcome sight.

"To what do I owe this uninvited visit?" I inquired stepping onto the porch.

"I just left a business meeting and I could not stop thinking of you. You're a distraction and I can't get you out of my mind. So here I am. Since you stood me up the other day for lunch and or dinner, I thought I'd try again today".

"Well Sir you have impeccable timing. Three minutes sooner I would have had to turn you down. It just so happens that I'm free." I said smiling

"Good. Get dressed" He replied.

"What, you mean I can't wear what I have on" I said jokingly. I was sporting a pair of cut off Syracuse sweatpants, that I had made into daisy dukes and a matching tee shirt.

"Give me 15 minutes and I'll be ready to go." I stated.

I was dressed to match his appropriate attire. I had on a white long strapless sundress with a pair of navy blue pumps and a matching clutch. I added an orange and multi blue color scarf to my neck for an added pop of color. Sprayed myself with some perfume, brushed my teeth, added a light coverage of makeup. He smiled as I entered the room. I think he was pleased at my choice of clothing. I twirled so that he could have the full picture. He stood there basking in my presence.

"A girl could get use to all this attention" I spoke

"There's always more for me to give, besides you should not have to compete for anyone's attention. Especially mines" he commented as he kissed my hand. We headed out the door and onto the busy Urban street. Again, many Buffalo Bills fans came out to look as they had become accustomed to the car or truck that Mr. Cornerback drove. But today he didn't even stop to sign an autograph. Today I had his full attention and I liked it. I wanted it. With eyes only deterring from me to watch the road, we pulled off just as I saw Que pulling up. He saw me and I just looked away. Now he knows what it's like to be in second place. We drove off, his hand on mine and it felt so natural.

Chapter Nineteen

"Treat Them Like They Want To Be Treated"
– Father MC

"Treat Them Like They Wanna Be Treated" Father MC

Ayanna

So the doorbell rang and for a moment my heart jumped. I wasn't sure if I wanted to go through with this. I prayed that Dade would not kill me or him before I had an opportunity to fuck him, I thought as I headed to the door. To my surprise. Dade had taken off. I didn't even hear him say goodbye or the door close behind him. Mental note to self, call someone to change your locks. I did not want to take the chance that in my foolishness I bring someone home and his ass walk in on us. The mere thought sent chills up my spine. I hope Sam looks as good as I imagined. He was sweaty earlier today and now I wanted to see the full package, all clean and neatly dressed. There was something about a guy that could dress that turned me on. The better they dressed the more likely they had cheddar, and you know me, money never hurt. Now don't get me wrong I make good money for a young black girl. I have no kids or other responsibilities, except taking care of me. But it is always better when someone else wants to do the job. That's what I loved about Dade. He always gave me a roll of paper to do whatever I wanted too with. He kept me laced and in turn I kept the house looking nice, meals on the table and the sex on point. In fact I oversaw all the properties and made sure shit stayed together. But if his ass can't get right, I'll have to turn all the way wrong.

I opened the door and there stood a tall chocolate piece of heaven. Sam was dressed to impress. He was wearing a tan linen pants suit. With a white v neck tee shirt underneath. He had on a pair of brown and white Stacy Adams sandals. He looked sharp. Delicious. He smelled like a light musk and my hormones went wild as I breathed his scent. It appears that great minds think alike as I was wearing a floral brown, red tan and white, strapless linen dress with a pair of red throng mule sandal that showed off my newly manicure toes and diamond ankle bracelet. I had curled my braids so that they cascaded down my back. My makeup was light but noticeable and my lips were outlined in a bold red. He smiled as I did at noticing each other.

He went in for a kiss on the cheek and asked if I was ready to go. I grabbed my purse, closed the door and set the alarm.

We went to Birchfields for Drinks. It was a much different crowd than I was used to seeing during the weekend. We talked and flirted, but I wanted to know what did that fudgesicle taste like. I drank 7 and Seven and he, Cognac on ice. I could tell with each sip of his drink he was wondering what I tasted like just as much as I was interested. The DJ was spinning some tunes and he grabbed my hand and we headed toward the back of the bar, when I noticed a familiar face.

Dade was seated in the corner of the club with the same chick that had come to the house earlier. I was hot!! That mutherfucker!! I wanted to scream. So that's why he did not say goodbye. So she's the reason I'm all in my feelings. I remained cool on the outside, but on the inside I was boiling. This was the first time we were seeing each other with random's. His random bitch looked at me and then at him. From the look on her face I assumed that she thought some shit was about to pop off. I just looked at her smiled and allowed my eyes to speak. My eyes said next time bitch. I'll see you next time. Dade however was wearing his anger on his face and sleeve. He had stopped being cozy with his bitch and now was all in my grill trying to see me. Now you wanna know what I'm doing. Now I got your attention, I thought. And since you wanna watch, I'll make sure to give you more than enough to think about. I smiled devilishly at him biting my lip. Game on!!

Sam and I danced. I allowed him to touch me and grind up on me, but seeing that we have captive audience, I felt it best to turn up the heat. I had requested the DJ play some Reggae. I do believe that it had been quite some time since Dade had seen me twirl my hips. I whined my body and ticked in my skin tight dress all over Sam's manhood. I slow whined and grinded on him in ways that mimicked Dade and I love making. I could see the fire in Dade's eyes. I could feel the daggers shooting me. The look on his face was enough to scare his bitch as she fought me for his attention to no avail. Sam grabbed my waist as I rolled back, up and down on his dick. I could tell he was enjoying it as I could feel him grow stronger and stronger. I danced as Dade and his crew watched in amazement. I danced as other onlookers wondered how I could move my body like that. The only person not happy about my performance was Dade. His crew was egging me on and I could hear them asking Dade if he was alright and not to sweat me. His bitch sat there studying my moves in envy. But it was too late. I struck a chord and I was gonna keep on playing.

We finished dancing and I was now ready to go. Dade had a few of is boys head outside. They left out the back door. I didn't want Sam to be injured because of anything I was doing, so I timed our exist as others were leaving. I finished the remainder of my drink while standing. Sam whispered in my ear how happy he was that we met today. I whispered back dido. Dade had not taken his eyes off me. I eyed him only when necessary which was to make sure he had not missed my performance. All of it. His fist were on the table balled up with aggression. Sam and I headed out the bar to the echo of Dade calling my name, "Ayanna!" "Ayanna!" You better not…Ayanna!! I heard glass breaking and chairs being thrown. Sam looked at me when we walked out the door with a puzzled look on his face. I smiled and kissed him. We headed to his car. I quickly got in and we drove away.

The score was now: Dade 0 / Ayanna 2.

Chapter Twenty

"Me So Horny"
— 2 Live Crew

"Me So Horney" 2 Live Crew

Monica

Damn. I was really hoping to get with Shawn. That nigga was packin' somethin special. I could tell by the way his gym shorts hugged his dick. The imprint it left in the mesh material and the way it swang as he ran up and down the basketball court. After talking to him for a minute, he told me that he had a girl and that they been together for a while. So I asked why was he all on me earlier? That nigga had the nerve to say he thought I was sexy and bold. Tell your bitch to be sexy and bold and maybe it won't be so easy for me to pull you away from her. The whole time I was talking, "What you girl got do with me?" It was sounding like a Positive K record. I finally had to just come out and say

"Shawn, I'm sure your girl is nice and all, but I don't give a fuck about your girl. You and her can play house all yall want. I aint tryna take her place, I aint tryna pay your bills, all I want to know is are we fucking tonight or what? Damn Nigga!" I said.

This bitch gonna say, "let me see if I can get away tonight".

I was like "you know what, lose my number". And I hung up on him. He gonna call me 20 minutes later talkin bout he can do it tomorrow. "Bye Nigga" I laughed. Aint nobody tryna fuck tomorrow, I'm tryna fuck tonight!

The phone rang again. This better not be that scared mutherfucka Shawn again. What his ass do, wait for that bitch to go to sleep and try to sneak out the hose, I thought laughing as I answered the phone.

"Wuz up who dis?" I asked

"Yo Monica it's "Rich and Mike, hope I wasn't disturbing you. Rich stated.

"Naw Rich you good, what yall up to tonight?" I asked trying to make small talk.

"Nothing much, I was callin to see if you wanted some company. We could stop by. I got the good good and a bottle. Thought we could just chill." Rich added

"Rich come through I replied. I was not going to pass up weed let alone a drink. Besides 2 out of 3 isn't bad I thought out loud.

I gave him my address and went to get ready for some company.

The doorbell rang. I escorted Rich and Mike down into the Batcave as me and my girls dubbed it. These niggas was acting like they had never seen a girl in her tee shirt and her panties. I was not about to throw on some clothes at 11 pm. It was still hot and humid outside and I was chillin'. If they could not handle it they were free to leave. Besides, I'm thinking these 2 really did not mind. They came with the blunts already to puff. I had brought down some glasses. I took some ice out the freezer that was located next to the washing machine and dryer in the far west corner of the basement. I sat there in the middle of them with my thong on and bra on. I took a puff of the Philly and passed it to Mike. We passed and puffed in our cypher. Now a bitch was real horney and hot. So I asked if it would be ok if I took off the rest of my clothes. You should have saw their eyes. It resembled middle schoolers at the thought of getting to 1st base. I undressed. We puffed and passed. I straight up asked who wants to eat my pussy and Mike jumped to the floor in between my legs and began to lick my pussy and eat me like I was a Twinkie. I puffed. I puffed and passed. Rich was watching Mike devour me as I made sounds of approval.

"Are you Jealous?" I asked Rich.

"Hell yeah" Rich eagerly stated. Awaiting his turn.

"Stand up and take off your clothes" I commanded.

Rich did just as I commanded. He stood there bare and his dick was thick and hard. It wasn't the biggest dick I had seen, but the girth was massive, like a beer can massive. It posed a challenge and I was going to conquer it. I pulled him to me and began to suck his dick like it was a pop can I was drinking from. He moaned, I moaned and Mike continued to lick and suck my pussy. There we were on the couch enjoying our high and each other.

We made our way to the bed in the back room of the basement. I took both their hands and lead them into the dark cool room. The only light coming through was that of the outside motion light from the garage through the egress window in the room. I instructed Rich to lay on his back and I climbed on top of him. I told Mike to come to me as I placed him in my month. I road and sucked as both men sang out loud in pleasure. I rode the width of his dick and allowed it to fill up my walls of my pussy. The girth pleased me but was not deep enough for me to really enjoy his dick. "I stopped sucking Mike's dick just shy of him exploding in my month. "Switch" I demanded. I was now riding Mike and enjoying the challenge of stretching my mouth around Rich's fat dick. It was beautifully thick and was just long enough to touch my tonsils. I grabbed his balls and rolled them in my hands. Because Rich's dick wasn't overpowering me in length it was easy for me to suck, lick and jerk him at the same time. I sucked his dick on the sides. I tongued and teased his head and spit all over his dick and made it moist enough for me to massage his balls and his shaft. I grabbed his ass and forced his massive width into my mouth as he moaned with excitement. I took him out of my mouth and had him sit on the edge of the bed. I finished riding Mike and asked him to massage the opening of my ass. He licked and fingered my ass as Rich began to eat my pusssy while I stood in front of him. I grabbed Mike's dick with my right hand and with the left I held onto Rich's dick. I messaged both of them as if I worked an assembly line and had mastered quality control. With each of them receiving equal attention and thrust of my hands, I could feel the precum squirt out as I caressed my fingers over the tips of their heads. It was a perfect game of patty cake. We were all hands on and each singing a verse of a nasty song. We sweated as the heat from our bodies made us want more and more. With each man kissing all over me, I began to shake in anticipation. I loved having this control over them. I loved that they were satisfying me. I loved knowing that I could handle both of them. I had Rich lay on his back I had Mike come in behind me. I held my ass and guided him into my opening. I then gently sat on Rich's dick and allowed them to work me. The thrusts from both of them caused a warming sensation in my body. I thanked them both as my body released my sweet juices all over their dicks. They rode me. I rode and bucked each of them.

I then pulled away from Mike and off of Rich. I lay on my back and told them both to enter me. I had Rich go first and then Mike. At first, I could tell they were uncomfortable with the idea, but I wanted both of them penetrating my pussy. I needed the width and the length to satisfy my carnal craving. I screamed for them to fuck me. And they did. In perfect rhythm, they beat my drum one after the other. They pounded my pussy. They pounded and I loved it. They pound and touched my body. I bucked back. They pounded one after another, dick to dick they entered me and touched the many nerves in my pussy. They beat and drummed me into ecstasy. We were high and free and fucking. I exploded all over them. I took both of them and sucked them one after another until they returned the favor. Rich exploded in my hand and Mike all over my chest. When we were done I tossed them a towel and had them clean off.

I wiped myself off. I went back into the front of the basement. Picked up a blunt, lit it and took a puff. They joined in. They were silent. No doubt trying to figure out what happen. I would give them a moment to process it and to catch their breath. Puff, puff, pass. Puff, puff, pass. Puff, puff pass. "You niggas ready for round 2?" I asked walking back to the bedroom ass naked and ready to fuck.

Chapter Twenty-One

"Who Got The Props"
— Black Moon

"Who Got the Props"- Black Moon

Dade

"Ayanna!" I screamed as she left the bar throwing my glass down breaking it. I stood up and grabbed Tammie by the arm. "Bitch lets go". I squared up the tab payed for the damage and we bounced. Outside I asked Beenie and Makin "which way did they go?" They did not notice them even leave the bar.

"Shit, Bumbaclot!!!" I screamed. Dis bitch done lost her goddamn mind I thought.

I looked down Main Street but without knowing what they rode up in, I was lost. As mad as I should be, I was impressed with Ayanna. I had never seen her with another, she got me all in my feelings wanting to shoot up da place. That bitch crazy. I smiled thinking of how good my babe looked. How her body moved to the beat of da music. She was fine. And the closest thing to the island for me. She was a bad bitch and to know that someone else was wit my babe had me steamin'. Plus she disrespected me. Showing out in front of me crew. Naaa that bitch is gunna learn. I thought as I drove off.

I dropped Tammie off at home. I warned her to stay away from me for a while. I could tell she was heartbroken at my response to seeing Ayanna. I hated what this was doing to her, but me and her were no more. Tammie knew that from the moment I met Ayanna, that things were different with her. Unlike the other girls that I use to mess with, Ayanna lasted, I grew to love her. I love her more than I ever could Tammie. Ayanna was my heart, but I just could not be a one woman man. It was not in my nature. Now look at me. It was for her protection and mine that I kept this secret hidden. I knew eventually I was going to have to explain Tammie to Ayanna. I just didn't think it would be like this.

Me wife and me girlfriend. Especially when Ayanna should be the one with my ring since she holds my heart.

I sat there in the dark. I sat on the couch at Ayanna's, waiting for her to walk thru the door. I waited. Minutes turned into hours. The dark became light and no still no Ayanna. I was boiling with anger and the thoughts of what and who she was doing made my heart harden. I sat there in silence and let my imagination run wild.

Ayanna

The look on that mutherfucka's face was priceless, I thought smiling to myself. We drove off so fast I was scared to look back to see if he actually came out of the bar to look for me. I showed his ass. I just knew that he was going to jump up and grab my ass and yoke me up, but that did not happen. I thought that he might have even shot Sam for touching on me, but he didn't. Maybe he doesn't care as much as I thought. There is no way I should have been able to leave that bar unscaved with me disrespecting him like that. Oh well. If he don't care then why should I? He can have that bitch hold him tonight and every night after that. I sat in silence holding back my tears. How could he? It doesn't matter now. What's done is done and now we both know.

I had been lost in my own thoughts and had not noticed that Sam had pulled up to his condo. We had driven all the way to Orchard Park and I had notice going through the toll booth. We got out of the car that was now parked in the garage. He opened the attached door that lead to the condo. I took off my shoes and walked on cream colored shag carpet. The condo was moderately decorated. The living room was anchored by a beige leather sofa set and 2 brown and cream micro-suede chairs. There was a sliding door covered in vertical blinds that lead to the patio.

"Make yourself a home" Sam invited. "Would you like something to drink?" he asked.

"Sure, what do you have" I inquired. "Better yet, just pour me something. Surprise me" I added.

I was standing at the patio doors overlooking the man made pond that adorned the landscape of the condo complex. I was busy in my thoughts and had not noticed that Sam was standing beside me holding a drink.

"So what's on your mind Ayanna?" he asked. "Would it have anything to do with the guy yelling for you at the bar tonight?" he added.

I turned around trying to act shocked, but could not hide my mixed emotions.

"Yes, it does. I'm so sorry." I confided.

"Hey Lady, we have all been there" he commented gently rubbing my shoulder.

"Tell me about it. I'm a good listener and I have a shoulder you can cry on" Sam said motioning me to join him on the sofa.

I sat there taking up his offer and began to explain what happen tonight and the events leading up to tonight. Sam was able to give me the man perspective to what was going on. Sam suggested that we speak to each other full disclosure. It seems that as much as we tried to not get too caught up in emotions we were. We thought we could have our cake and eat it too and no one would get hurt. But we both seem to be hurting now.

Sam and I talked a lot. He shared with me his last relationship and why it did not work. And how playing games lead to his losing the one person he actually loved. So he was speaking from experience. We talked about our goals and our futures. We talked about what we both wanted in a relationship and why it was so hard for us as men and women to be so honest with each other. It felt good and refreshing. It was not the normal sex'em and leave date. We talked for hours and did not even realize that it was 3am in the morning. He asked me to stay, no strings attached. I slept next to him in his King size bed. He held me tight and for the first time in a long time I felt safe. I felt free and I felt like this was something I deserved. A man who could love me for me. A one woman man for a one man women. But damn, that fudgesicle sure would have been nice.

Chapter Twenty-Two

"Deep Cover"
– Dr. Dre Ft Snoop Dog

Deep Cover- Dr. Dre ft. Snoop Dogg

Jay

"Man, I got Yazz. We're heading to the spot. I'm going to keep her there for a while until we get this thing under wraps. I'll hit you up later. Peace." I spoke and ended the conversation.

We need to handle this shit before anyone gets hurt. I can't believe we did not see this coming. We've been so wrapped up in these females that we were blinded. This can never happen again. It's so not like me or Que to have our guards down. After what happen with Anika we should've known better. But if they think we just gonna let this shit go they have another thing coming. I promised myself that I would never allow anything to happen to Yazz. I smiled looking at her. We were heading to my house off of Sheridan and Colvin. I had all of Yazz's things brought over to the house. I picked up a few groceries to get us by for now. I did not feel comfortable taking Yazz back to my apartment in the city. I needed to remove her from whomever was following her. Plus niggas wasn't gonna be coming out here starting no shit. The white police officers out here don't play. More than 2 niggas in a vehicle and they pulling you over. I knew I was going to have to explain this shit to Yazz. I promised her no secrets and I don't intend to start lying now.

We arrived at the safe house. I parked the car in the garage and we headed into the house. I hugged Yazz and promised that I will take care of her. I promised that I will not allow anything to happen to her. I sat her down and explained everything. There was little surprise to anything I had disclosed to her. She looked worried, but not afraid. She understood. We were heading for war and there was no holding back.

Que

"Yo who the fuck was that Anika just left with?" I asked a dude who was posted up watching them drive off.

"He plays for the Buffalo Bills, cornerback I believe," he replied

"Thanks my man" we dabbed up and I got back in the car and drove off.

Damn it Anika! "What the fuck are you doing Ma?" I yelled hitting the steering wheel. "I know Jay told you to stay put", I said aloud shaking my head.

"Que. Yo shorty will be safe for now. I know that dude is high profile these niggas out here won't try anything when she with him", I said to myself trying to calm my nerves.

Now all I have to do is take care of business. You need to focus. Handle this shit and then go get your girl. For now you need to make sure everyone is safe. I need to deal with these punk muthafucka's. Either they gone kneel or they gone lay. If they want war, Imma bring it them.

Chapter Twenty-Three

"Have You Ever Loved Somebody"
— Freddie Jackson

"Have You Ever Loved Somebody"- Freddie Jackson

Anika

What a wonderful day. We had lunch at Salvatore's. Then went all the way downtown to walk along the waterfront. We had ice cream and just talked. We walked and talked. About everything. I have never made a connection with anyone quite the way I have with him. He's here, with me, no beepers, no games. This is different. Strange. I'm not sure how I should feel with him. All I know is Que's not here. He's always late or leaving me early. I just can't. Girl just enjoy the moment. If it's meant to be then it will be.

We drove back to his place. He asked what would I like to do tonight. I told him we should go out. Crawdaddy's would be jamming. I told him to call a few of his friends and tell them to meet us there. I needed to release some stress. With everything that was going down with Yazz, I could not help but think it had something to do with Que and Jay. I needed to just let go and have a carefree night. I haven't seen Monica or Ayanna in days let alone talk to them. So a night out was long overdue. Mr. Cornerback told me that he invited 3 of his boys one being the guy Monica had fucked with. He asked if she would be joining us because his boy hadn't seen her and he was feignin' for her. We laughed. We took the drive back to his place. I washed up and choose an outfit that we had purchased on one of our shopping sprees. I walked out of the bedroom dressed in a pair of faux leather pants that hugged my curves and accentuated my small waist and rounded hips. My ass looked good too. I paired it with a white lace shirt that buttoned only to my midriff and exposed the navel. It was long sleeve and was airy. I wore a pair of Black patent leather peep toe 5inch stilettos. The heel to the shoes was a cork, brown material. They were hott!! I knew I looked good, but the look on his face was priceless. It was like I could not disappoint him. Like every time he saw me he was in awe. I felt special. He was wearing a pair of perfectly creased dark jeans, a crisp tee and a plaid blazer. He looked very GQish. I smiled

"Nice" I commented.

"You not the only person who clean up good" he jokingly replied.

"I'm almost done. I just need to find some earrings and to finish my makeup and I'll be ready to go." informed him.

Anika, your already damn fine, any more and I'll have to fight every dude in the club to prove myself to you he busted out laughing.

"Well you have to do it, cause you know I got the good ishh!" I laughed.

"Damn right" he said looking at me watching my every move.

We arrived at Crawdaddy's. The parking lot was full and there was a small line out front with people waiting to get in. We walked up just in time. Monica, Erika and Yvette were all standing prim proper and hood. My girls. They did not disappoint. They heard ballers and they showed up and out ready for a good time. Ayanna is coming but she was bringing someone. She said we would talk later and she would fill me in. I introduced everyone to my date. That's funny, I have a date, I thought smiling on the inside.

"My friends will thank you" he whispered in my ear.

"What you thought, I had ugly friends", I laughed!!!

He took my hand and walked me into the club. All of us cut the line and walked right on in. Mr. Cornerback had reserved the

VIP section of the bar. We walked upstairs to the reserved area. We made introductions. His friend's eyes lit up like kids in the candy store. I remembered their familiar faces from the first night me and Mr. Cornerback spent together. These were his friend that got to see me model his tee shirt. Monica had already rekindled her 2week romance with Mr. Wide Receiver. They had already gone off into their own little corner and were kissing on each other. Erika and Yvette made real nice with the other Pro Bowlers they just met. The defensive player was all into Erika. And he should be. Erika was light bright and damn near white. I assumed she was mixed, although she never mentioned her father. He must be the black in her coffee, because that chick had bad black bitch tendencies! She had fine long curly hair that she straighten for tonight. Erika had on a pair of light colored jeans and a matching tube top that tied in the back. She wore a pair of hot fuchsia platform stilettos that wrapped around her ankle. She stood 5'3" but in her heels she was tall enough to dance with the dudes without them having to get to low. She was cute. The ballers were ordering bottles as the music and cheers from below filled the club. The DJ gave out mad shout outs to the Players in VIP. We cheered and toasted up. Not before long, Ayanna and her mystery date showed up and joined us. She introduced us to Sam. He was nice. He was also different than the island niggas she normally went for. Plus she was smiling, which was rare for her when around some dude. Yvette was cozied up with the other Mr. Wide Receiver. He seemed to be enjoying her company. Yvette had these captivating hazel gray eyes.

Her and Yazz were cousins. She was hella cool just like Yazz. And just like Yazz, she had legs for days, medium size titts and a small ass. She had shoulder length hair and wore it parted down the middle. She too was dressed to impress. Yvette sported a pair of leather short rompers that showed off her legs. The jumper was a long sleeve one piece that she had unbuttoned to her navel. She wore a black lace bra. She topped the look off with a pair of leopard print heels. We were all fly. Besides I don't hang with no torn up bitches.

We were on the dance floor. The crowd was wild. The DJ was spinning the latest tunes. "Aint nothing but a G Thang" by Dr. Dre began to play and crowd got hyped. The DJ kept the party going. He added "Whoop There It Is" by Tag Team and the girls went crazy. It was like he was calling all the ladies to the dance floor to get ready for the great ass shaking contest. 2 Live Crew "It's Ya Birthday" was next and we went wild. I could see Mr. Cornerback watching me from the balcony. I motioned for him to join me. But he watched. He watched like I was performing a play on Broadway. And I performed.

"All I wanna do is zooma zoom, zoom, zoom and boom boom!!" the crowd chanted to Wreckx n' Effect. All the Guys in the club had enclosed the ladies on the dance floor so that they could watch us shake our asses. Some guy got behind me and started dancing. Not to be out done I accepted his invitation and started freaking him. Now I don't mind freaking someone I don't know but it was something about this dude. He was rough he kept coming for me, and the look in his eyes was almost of hate rather than fun and enjoyment. I tried backing off of him but he grabbed me. I pulled away and he must have gotten mad because he rose up. Before I knew what was going down, Mario one of Ques boys had punch the shit out of him. He looked at me and told me to leave. Now! All I heard was the dude yell out "if you fuck with her you end up dead! That bitch is going down", he continued. Mario went to town on that nigga. The security guards had to rush the crowd and take Mario off of him. The music had stopped playin and everyone was backed against the wall. Mr. Cornerback had made his way to me and grabbed me and escorted me out of the Club. Ayanna, Sam, Monica and the team followed suit. He placed me in the car and told everyone he was getting me out of here. I was in shocked. Shocked at what that nigga yelled at me and in shock of seeing Mario there. He normally did not frequent those types of places. Why was he there? Who was the guy I was dancing with? How did he know about me, about Bam? Did Mr. Cornerback hear what he said? I was so confused. But I know one thing for sure, that nigga came for me. What I didn't know was who sent him and why. The only thing I wanted right now was "Que" I whispered looking out the window as we drove off.

Chapter Twenty-Four

"Don't Be Afraid"
– Aaron Hall

"Don't Be Afraid" Aaron Hall

Que

I got the call about what happened at the Crawdaddy's about 1:30am. I sent Tony and Big Mitch to go handle that nigga and find out who sent him after Anika. I can't believe this shit. Mario told me that she left with ol' boy. Good. He'll protect her for now anyway. But I'll handle if from here. On my way to meet up with Tony and Big Mitch, I'm driving down the 33, weaving in and out of traffic. I take it back down town and pull off headed toward High Street. I take a few lefts and rights and I arrive at my destination. They got this nigga in the basement tied up like a piñata. They were taking turns beating that mutherfucka like his blood was candy and they wanted more. They filled me in on some of the details they were able to get out of him. I was satisfied. It was enough information for me to put some more of the missing puzzle pieces together. These dudes fuckin' with the wrong one. And to try to get at me through Anika? Fuck Naw!

I finished that mutherfucka off and left them to clean up. Before the night is over, I'm sure my hands were going to get even dirtier.

Anika

I lay there in the bed thinking of the events of last night. I'm laying in this man's bed, in his house, and all I wanted was Que. The only thing that can put me at ease is the person that has protected me from the beginning. With him I am never worried. With him I know nothing will ever happen to me. I'm sure by now he knows about last night. I need to talk to him. I need to know why this is happening. I just need him. First thing I'm going to do when I leave here is page him and let him know to meet me. Yes, that's what I'll do.

Mr. Cornerback came back into the bedroom with arms full. He made me tea and breakfast in bed. He was so sweet. He was so caring, but he was not Que. And right now I needed my protector. I smiled. We kissed and I thanked him. I was not really hungry, but I ate something. He held me. It was comforting. But all the muscles in his well defined arms could not compare to the comfort and security that Que's presence gave me. He took the breakfast tray away. I could tell he wanted to talk about last night. So I started the conversation. He was rubbing my feet and I asked

"So you have questions about last night"

He looked up at me with a perplexed look on his face.

"No, I don't have any questions. I know you have a life outside of me and what we do" he calmly stated. "All I want to know is are you ok. You're my only concern right now. I told you when we first hooked up I got you. I meant that I got you. I know what you're about, and I'm ok with that. And if I'm going to stand by your side I need to be alright with everything. So no Anika, I don't want to know anything unless you want to share." he commented staring me in the eyes.

I melted. I knew he understood. I just wasn't ready to open up to him just yet. No one knew everything about me except Que. And even he didn't know all the details. I wanted to let him in. I wanted to trust in him and whatever we were doing, but I held back. I just couldn't. I kissed him gently and he held me. We didn't need words. The silence was enough for me to know I'm catching feelings, but I'm already in love and anything that happens with Mr. Cornerback is just adding fuel to a burning heart. Now I'm just confused, catching feelings for someone who should have just been a short term good time and chasing after someone that may not want me. Afraid and confused. Anika girl get it together I whispered to myself.

Chapter Twenty-Five

"Changes I've Been Going Through"
— Mary J. Blige

"Changes I've Been Going Through"- Mary J Blige

Yazz

I rarely left the house these days without Jay. Even when I went to work, Jay had someone posted up in the parking lot watching over me. Things are getting thick. I can only overhear bits and pieces of conversations between Que and Jay, but from what I knew they were in the heat of it. War.

I suppose this was the lifestyle. I understood, but I didn't. To me there was enough of Buffalo to go around and enough feigns for everyone to be prosperous. And with Jay's background you would think that he knew that. That he knew there was a better way. Every day I waited for some horrible news like he had been shot or Que was injured or even worse one of my girls was dead. I couldn't think about that shit. It will drive you crazy. The mind is a dangerous tool in dreaming up what ifs and right now I needed to live in the here and now. Jay did not want any of the girls coming out to the house for now. He wanted to make sure that the spot remained tight and we stayed safe. I spoke with them almost every day. If it wasn't Monica it was Ayanna or Anika. They filled me in on the drama that happened at Crawdaddy's the other night. I knew that Jay heard about it. I overheard him and Que talking about it. All I knew was that it was taken care of. I knew better than to ask any questions. I knew what that meant and me overhearing that was more than enough for me.

I was becoming lost in Jay's world. Almost suffocating. I wanted out of his world, but I wanted him. And for him I would stay. I would stay and endure the danger and ignore the consequences. Dammit! God, let this shit be over soon. Let everyone come out of this ok, I prayed. Even though God had let me down so many times before, I needed this to be over with soon and for life to get back to normal.

Chapter Twenty-Six

"Wu-Tang Clan Aint Nuttin Ta F' Wit"
—Wu-Tang Clan

Wu-Tang Clan Aint Nuttin Ta F' Wit" -Wu-Tang

Que

I met up with Jay, Mario and the family. I needed updates and quick. I was gettin push back from the family on why it was taking so long to move product into the Bailey district of the East Side. They were aware of the few hiccups but we needed these blocks to be up and running asap. I bought us a few days but by the end of the week we needed to square this shit away. I needed eyes and feet on the street.

We had finalized our next steps. Everything was going according to plan. It had already been a very busy summer. The heat was on in more ways than one. We didn't need fuckups with this job. Members of the family were sent in to handle business in the Kerr and Winslow area a few months back and resulted in more than enough bodies and arrests to flag street activity on the rise. Anytime shit make the Eyewitness News and the Buffalo News Paper we weren't quiet enough and when you aint quiet you makin' noise. Noise leads to arrest and that equals loss profits and jail time. And I don't fucks with that. Besides my crew be on point. You wouldn't know if we didn't want you to. Besides I don't roll with weak ass bitches. I keep that shit tight just like my reputation. Everything that go down happens because I said so. And nothing happens in these streets without me knowing first. Even when niggas try, I know what cookin' before shit pop off. I squash that shit before they even know what happens. The FAM aint no joke, you don't fuck with them or me.

"Who the fuck is paging me like this" I said out loud passing the pager to Jay to see if he recognized the number.

He shook his head "Naw. Bruh" he said handing it back to me.

I pulled over to use the payphone. I called the number back.

"Que this is Ant, spot number 3 was just hit. They shot up the place and killed Tone and Mel. I just cleaned up the spot, I got everything out. What you want me to do? Cops be here in about 3".

"Get the fuck out of there meet me at dungeon" commanded and hung up the phone.

"Fuck"!! I screamed getting back into the car, pulling a 180 and headed in the opposite

Direction. Jay looked at me like he knew it wasn't good news. He paged everyone to meet us at the dungeon asap. That nigga already knew. We been in the game too damn long for us not to be able to read each other's minds. That nigga was my brother for life. I had his back and he had mine. And tonight we was gone need that brotherhood to make sure we came out of this shit unscaved.

Jay

I set the table up. The dungeon was set up like a military artillery bunker. Everything you needed to get down and dirty was there. I laid out everything we would need. I had bullet counts, vest, mask, gloves and a gun selection that would make a 5 Star General piss his pants if he knew we rolled the streets better than his most skilled soldiers. It was war and we were prepared. Que was over in the corner looking at maps and planning how we were going to do this. Get in and out with no issues. I knew that nigga was thinking nasty. They needed to know that we weren't fuckin' playin' no more. The hit was coming with a loud Bang.

The crew was in line, they already knew. We each picked our poison. Made sure we had clips and backups. Untraceable. All in black. We headed out in groups based on our talents. We had a few wanna be sharp shooters already in position. We were ready for some action. The music of a hard beat and bass jump started the adrenalin. Car 1 pulled up, Car 2 pulled up, 3,4, 5,6,7 and 8 all at their designated hit. The time was 8:30 pm and at 8:35 there wasn't a soul alive at those spots. Body count 31. 3 street corners hit and 3 dope houses. We took the product, cash and the weapons.

No confirmation that Punk-ass nigga Mike or Rich were among the deceased. That's ok. We got something special planned for them 2 anyway. We were in and out with only minor wounds. With more than two thirds their crew taken out, that more than makes up for their punk ass hit earlier today. We would finish the battle by night's end and Bailey would be ours.

Chapter Twenty-Seven

"Straight Up Menace"
— MC Eight

Straight Up Menace- MC Eight

Monica

I knew them niggas couldn't handle sharing me. Eer' since the threesome they been actin up. Now I can't spend time with one without the other one catchin feelings. Niggas! Who says they aint sensitive!? I laugh out loud. I sat there watching Mike and Rich argue over some bullshit.

"Aint y'all supposed to be boyz" I spoke out loud.

"Monica shut yo ass up" Rich said as he took a puff of the blunt we had just rolled.

"We used to be tight till yo ass" Mike laughed out loud. "Now you got us measuring dicks and shit talcumbout who shit is bigger? You a bad bitch Monica. That's real". Mike puffed and exhaled.

"You know me. We can do that shit all day, but on the low Rich, Mike got the bigger dick" I laughed out loud, "Yours thicker tho" I finished.

We all laughed.

There were about 6 other niggas in the cut. They each had a chick by they side. No one better than me. They was hoodrats fah real.

You could hear that West Coast shit bumpin' in the background, as the billiards game was going. A few people were playing dominos. It was a real live spot. They kept the drinks flowing and the Phillies stuffed. The air was thick as hell as we smoked one after another.

I was listening to the music and just chillin'. Even if you weren't smoking, your contact high was just a strong. We were all high. Every once and a while a pager would go off, but nothing that broke the vibe of the cypher. We cracked jokes. On the tv we were watching Bill Bellamy's 15th Young Comedians Special. We started talking about bungee jumping! We were high as hell, cause aint no way our black asses would ever sign up for that shit.

"Rich you can bungee jump with my dick" Mike said and we burst out laughing.

"Fuck you Mike" Rich commented.

I laughed so hard.

"Hey where's the bathroom in the place?" I asked some chick pointed to the back of the hallway by the back door. I excused myself. I noticed the time it was 2 mins to 11pm. I went to the restroom pissed, and checked myself in the mirror. Still fly as hell I thought. I lit the blunt I had taken off the side table. Took a puff. Exhaled. And Out the back door I went without anyone noticing.

Que

Received the page at 9:30 and 10. Every half hour like clockwork. Good. It was 2 minutes to 11. We pulled up to the spot. No one was on the corner. By the time Mario opened the door to the spot My clock read 11pm. And like I was clockin' in time for a job, we lit that shit up. Sprayed the entire place from the front. Jay and his crew rolled in from the back. All you saw was sparks of light that painted bodies in red. We did not even give them a chance to fire back. The element of surprise. I saw one after another fall, taking their last breath. Niggas & bitches, one, two three to the floor. Glass. Walls. Bodies. The smell of blunts hung over us heavy and it could have been easy to miss someone. We thorough as hell though. Checked everyone. Shot twice, three times. Execution style. On the couch sat Mike and

Rich. Looking like fragments of their former selves. Blood dripped out of Mike's mouth. Eyes wide open. Blunt in hand. Surprise the look on his face. Damn. Too bad. Rich was reaching for his piece. Caught one through the side of his chest, another through his stomach, another through his arm, one through his head. Can't tell which one was the shot that did him in. He was slumped over sporting a fresh blood stained fade, and a blood soaked tee. Gold choked his neck as he sat lifeless.

Jay was getting ready to make like we weren't there. The fire was blazing and we were out. Just as quick as we rolled in we scattered like roaches in many directions. Ditched and burned vehicles. Clothes changed.

Already at the next spot. Took a drink. Waited for Jay and Mario to report. Took another shot. One and then another. Reports favorable. We toast. We each headed off in different directions. Me to report back the FAM. Jay to clear the dungeon and Mario to make payments. The price of War aint cheap, but it is well worth it. And as promised, we delivered the Bailey territory and those corners now repped the FAM.

Chapter Twenty-Eight

"Rebirth Of Slick (Cool Like Dat)"
Digable Planets

"Rebirth of Slick (Cool Like Dat) "- Digable Planets

Monica

I woke up feeling rested. I went to the kitchen cut up a grapefruit into sections. Added a shake of granulated sugar. Toasted up a half of bagel and topped it off with peanut butter. A cup of lipton tea with a swirl of honey, pipin` hot steamed from my mug as I turned on the TV. I was able to catch the last 15 minutes of the news on channel 7. I heard the weather forecast for the day and the next. Good I thought. I was headed out needed to get my hair done today and get ready for tonight. It was club night and I needed something new to rock tonight. Needed to extra. I needed a new set of players to add to the repertoire. I was eating my grapefruit when Don Postles of Eyewitness News started recapping the horrific events of last night

"Last NIght the city's east side turned into a war zone as suspected drug dealers and their crews were gunned down in cold blood. There were multiples sites throughout the eastside reporting gun violence. The body count stands at 25 confirmed dead. This brutal slaughter brings the summers total to 210 murders since the start of this year, with more than half of that happening during the humid summer. This is turning out to be the deadliest summer on record. Stay tune for more on this deadly and sad plague that is hitting our city"

They showed several prime areas of the eastside mostly the Bailey area. I recognized those areas. I knew them well. How sad I thought. But that's the life. If you're not willing to accept the consequences then don't do the crime. Besides the streets don't cry for no one. I thought as I finished my breakfast.

I got dressed and headed out the door. I needed to hurry, I was running late for my hair appointment. When I arrived at

DeAndre's the salon was busy. Thank goodness my stylist was finishing up with her client. I was next. There was mega gossip being discussed. I just sat there and laughed. Half was true and the other half who knows. It was busy talk and I enjoyed it everyone was commenting on the latest shooting. Big Mike and Rich and their crews were known in these parts. They were hood legends. Some were speculating others were sad. Someone asked me how I felt being I knew them. I just shook my head. Not my fight I thought. Not my worry.

By the time I was done, I had a fresh new do, and managed to to catch up on all the latest hood drama. Off to the boutique for something that matched the new do.

I got back in my car and there was a package. Just as promised. I took a peek. All about the Benjamins baby!I smiled and thought Dick, Money and Weed all a bitch needs!!

Chapter Twenty-Nine

"Sucka Nigga"
– A Tribe Called Quest

"Sucka Nigga" -Tribe Called Quest

Jay

I made sure Mario did his part. He checked in. All was good. The dungeon was clean and locked up. Que was good and so was I. We had new feet and eyes on the street. The block was hot, but it was our block now. The FAM had expanded. Hopefully this was it for now. But all they needed to do was say the word and the next fight was on. We control the majority of the city. And the neighborhoods that we didn't walk at least got product from us. Like I said we owned the City. This was good. The FAM saw Que and myself as capable which meant business was good. Everyone was happy except the cops and the news. They wanted the blood shed to end. It'll end when we're done. Just one one issue at hand. Whoever was stalkin Yazz and Anika still needed to be dealt with. They were next. It was only time before they messed up. And we'll be there to clean that shit up.

Que

Anika has been paging me. I gotta make time to connect with her. I hate that this life does this to her. But she knows. The Streets own me. Plus she FAM. I don't care what she say. FAM comes first. But Damn. At least I can check in. She know, she'll always have my heart. My pockets however will fahever be loyal to the FAM. Dude thats fucked up I thought, but the truth.

The FAM was in place. It was like we have alway been there. We left no trace of that Bailey Crew. You can't hide from the FAM. Even with Po po searchin, most of them on the cut. The FAM is tight with it. Besides they can search but we clean, not a trace of evidence. Not cocky, just truth. Anywho, on to the next. Finish off whoever is messin with mines. It's just a matter of time. They better hope they get me on a good day. Because I'm takin out families, bitches & niggas. Pray I'm feeling nice, cause you fuckin with the wrong one. And if you didn't know, your soon to find out.

I pull into GIGi's and order the usual. I always set in the back of the restaurant facing the door. My back is never to the door. I need to see everything. Account for everyone that crosses my path. I'm uncomfortable with suck niggas coming up to me like they know me. Shid they don't know me, they know the legend. The shadow that roams the street. People knew that, know not a cent more. I sat there eatin. Before long Jay showed up. I order his plate it was coming out just as he sat down. We made plans to get up with the girls. He said Yazz was getting jittery being on lockdown. Cool I thought I will give me a chance to get with Anika. We would meet up tonight at the club. This would send a message that we ain't worried or scared. Show yourself whoever you are.

Chapter Thirty

"Body And Soul"
– Anita Baker

"Body and Soul" - Anita Baker

Yazz

I ran the water in the shower. The temperature was just right. I undressed and stepped in. I was being guarded by 2 enormous rottweilers, Ren and Akil. they kept me company whenever Jay was not home or I could not find anyone to talk too. I was finally relaxing. I heard the door to the garage open. That could only mean one thing Jay was home. Plus my hairy protectors did not bark. They were well trained.

"I'll be right out" I called out

Before I could even say another word Jay was naked joining me in the shower. He looked stressed and tired. But there was a sense of calm about him today. I smiled. He smiled back. I turned back around and allowed him to hold me.as the water dripped over us. He kissed me. My neck, My shoulders. My ears. Switching from on side to the other. I moaned. He held me with one hand as he pulled on my damp hair. I opened my legs to welcome him home. We stood there in the steam me pressed up against the glass shower door making designs into the condensation that built up on the doors from the heat of the water. He found me and entered me with the talents of an artist and I was his clay. Molding my body to conform to whatever position he desired. He loved me soft and fucked me hard. I held his legs as he pressed deep into me. My grip slipping with every pounce he grafted. I love it. I treasured having him control me like this. I moaned. I sacrificed my body for him to worship. He placed his fingers in my mouth. I sucked his digits mimicking the actions of pleasuring his manhood. I came over and over again.He held me as my body shook from the artistic delights he created within me. His dick hung to the left. It curved so that with each thrust he hit uncharted spots of pleasure I had never knew until him. He moaned. I gently pulled away from him and locked eyes with him. He watched as I lowered myself I allowed the water to cover me as I sucked his dick. I took him all in. I massaged him like I missed it. Like a long lost friend. I loved sucking him. The flavor of his cum excited me. It was the fuel that fed my soul. I longed for it. I sucked and sucked as his knees weakened, as he gripped helplessly the wet wall with little support . It was as if we tag teamed him to succumb to us, to me. Begged him to release all his pain, heartache and forbidden things. I jammed his cock deep into my voice. I gave it sound. It excited him. I could feel his dick grow within me and compulsed with pleasure. I was satisfied as I drank his gift. I kissed him and he pulled me on him. He held me with my legs wrapped around his waist. He inserted himself into me. I straddled him. I rode him until the water became lukewarm. We ended on the bathroom floor exhausted and relieved. I had managed to wash the days weight off of him. I knew this life had taken him to dark places. I hoped that I provided a source of light and comfort for him. In silence we lay on the bathroom floor. Nothing else needed to be said. I rinsed the horrors of the street away. He was free to love for now. I was free to be loved.

Chapter Thirty-One

"Give It Up Turn It Loose"
– En Vogue

"Give it up, turn it Loose"- En Vogue

Ayanna

Sam has truly been heaven sent. He was a good man. I did not deserve his kindness. I had been camped out at his house for the last few days. We talked. About everything. He had me thinking about things and ideas I had not given much thought too. No question was off limits. He was worldly and I was hood. We made the perfect pair. He did not judge me. He was actually impressed. I told him about me. The whole truth. The honest truth. And in turn I was finding myself. My worth. I was only going to be young for so long and my beauty my body would only last for so long, what was my end game. There was always someone prettier, with a better "it" body, tricks, although the same, the game won't change just the names and faces. I wanted more. I wanted something different. This mutherfucker had me and we ain't even fuck yet.

Everyday I woke up in his arms. I felt free. I felt loved. I felt truly as though he were my own, not to share. We ate breakfast together, we talked. He even bathed with me. And as tempting as it was when touched and nothing more.

This must be that shit Ankia and Yazz be on. Having niggas do all this fancy shit for them. But I must admit, this would not happen with Dade. Lord know the sex was good. Damn good. Put his lies. The guilt in his eyes. The way I knew now I would never be his. I've dated enough married men in my day to know they never walk away. There was only one that came close, AJ.

AJ and I started off as the Uncle of a dear friend of mine. He was nice looking for a mature man. I was 18 at the time barely legal. I watched how he cared for his family. I loved the way he looked at his wife. I loved that he loved with little in return. One day while visiting my friend who stayed with his family. I noticed his demeanor was different. He held a beer in hand and was pacing as if something was ailing him. In an empty room, he spoke to me.

"Never get married" he said looking at me with intense eyes.

I smiled sadly that his pain was so real. I asked "Why"

He began to explain to me the hurt and pain that came along with loving someone with the thought of death do you part and them having that person you took a solemn vow with in front God, family and friends only to have them betray you, that love and trust.

She cheated. I saw her, laying there fucking another man I saw her face and the joy he brought her. I watched the years of our marriage wash away as he humped her, I saw my love for her turn to hate as she allowed herself this forbidden pleasure. I watched as she returned home to me cook my dinner as if nothing happen. She kissed our children with the same month she wrapped around his dick. I watched for days how she betrayed me and our vow. I watched until my heart harden. I told her today that I knew. I told her to end it. But I don't know why. I'm not sure why I told her to do that. It felt like the right thing to say and do. Honorable. But truth, I don't love her. I don't think I ever did. We had just been together for so long that it seems like the right thing to do. So we did. Marry. Kids came and years went by and I think I confused loyalty with love. I was fond of her. But I don't think it was love.

I sat there listening to his pain. I sat there waiting for my friend to return. She had driven her mother to work and did not have room for me in the car. I stayed behind and allowed myself be a pawn in destiny's game. I sat there as he looked at me. I had seem that look before from men. I was a temptation. AJ was no different. I watched as he sat the beer bottle down and walked to the back of the house. I watched as he looked back at me. I followed with my eyes until my body followed suit. He lead me down the hall and into a bedroom. He undressed me long after he undressed me with his eyes. I lay on his bed. In a bed reserved for someone with titles of Mr and Mrs. I lay there as he opened my legs and kissed my inner thighs. He made his way to my garden and watered it with his tongue. It was pleasure that I had never felt before. My back arched to greet his tongue making circles strumming me like strings to his violin. Echoing his pain as if he was a soloist playing a sad version of love and heartbreak. I cried out in pure ecstasy as he gave himself to me. He sucked me until I had nothing left to give. He held me as he caressed my thighs and sat there between my legs as if I was braiding his hair. He kissed my legs, and sucked my toes making eye contact with me with each toes he whispered too.

I wanted to return the favor. I wanted to release the pain this man was holding on too. I sat on his lap facing him. I wrapped my legs around him gently placing his manhood in me. I rode him and held him as the tears road down his face. I whispered everything was going to be ok. He held me as our bodies composed a symphony of melodic tones. With each bounce my body thrusted into him, he held me tighter and tighter. It was angelic and demonic at the same time. It was the good and bad battling for love. It was pain personified and pleasure restored. We gave hope in an unforgivable act. Without words our worlds collided. I held him and he thanked me.

It was the beginning of what could have been a beautiful relationship. He loved me and I loved him. We spent every available opportunity with each other. I became the constant in his world. I should him what love reciprocated looked and felt like. He showered me with gifts. I was thankful. He became a part of my circle of friends. We were a couple. We were well on our way to being Man and Wife or so I thought. The only role I would play was fool. Not long after we were close to celebrating our 1 year anniversary, his wife or soon to be ex wife shows up. She's pregnant. She announces that the child is his. I laugh as I know this not to be true. He had been with me for almost a year. I was fulfilling his desires, what purpose would he have for her anymore. I was confused as he looked at her and could not rightly deny her claims. I felt my heart ache, I felt my breath heavy. He tried to explain. I could not listen. At first I begged him to forget about her. And for a while he did. Until the baby came. Them there was the constant communication between the two. Then there was the late nights. Them there was the we're trying to work things out and I was standing in the way conversation. I cried. That same pain he felt he had now given to me. My first heartbreak, My first of many things, married men, oral sex, thoughts of marriage all wiped clear as I left. I left him with the promise that she will do it again. Hurt him. And she did. The baby not his. She cheated several time on him again and again she did not even try to hide her indiscretions. She inflected darts of pain and agony that aged him 10 years. I was happy and sad. He tried to return to me but I couldn't' accept him. His hardened heart left him a shell of his former self. One I could not recognize or love.

I was done with that lesson. I was forever shaped by the love and pain AJ had shared with me. I would use this fucked up measurement as the guideline for future relationships. My love them and leave them attitude. My keep your bitches to the left, 'cause I'm at your right motto, me dealing with half truths and the fear of knowing love pure love and acceptance. All stem from AJ. This reason allowed me and Dade to continue for so long. I wanted to Mature and grow. I wanted love. I knew this would never happen with Dade. It would continue to be one fight after another and one lie to cover another. It was time to confront my mess I created. It was time but I knew Dade wouldn't give up without a fight.

Chapter Thirty-Two

"Neither One Of Us"
– Gladys Knight

"Neither One of Us" -Gladys Knight

Ayanna

I had informed Sam that I would be going home tonight. So after a very delicious dinner- The man can cook! Sam gathered my belongings and drove me home. He walked me in and made sure everything was ok. He made sure that I had set the new security passwords and the my new keys worked ok. He held me tight and kissed me goodnight. I promised to call him first thing in the morning. Besides I knew he would be back here tomorrow afternoon as we made plans. I smiled as I watched him drive off. He was the welcome I needed, needed and longed for. The new beginning I deserved.

I was busy cleaning up the house. I unpacked my belongings and was ready to soak in the tub. I declined the opportunity to join the crew for a night out on the town. I needed to rest. I knew that Dade was coming, and a fight was going to happen. I was mentally prepared, but emotionally I could never fully prepare for that kind of warfare.

I sat there in my bedroom refreshed after a glass of wine and a nice warm bath. I was staring at the room. Looking at all of Dade's belongings. I packed them up. One by One I cleared his memory from my room. Clothes,Pictures, personal items. I packed up everything. It was time to say goodbye. I thought it best to mail the items to him. I did not want any of our usual drama. You know the cuss each other out tell the neighborhood, call the policy kind of bull shit we norally did. I wanted him to go calmly into the night so I could have my moment in the sun.

I was finished with the packing. I walked back downstairs to the kitchen. I was pouring a glass of wine. I failed to notice the answering machine. It was lit up flashing an absurd number of missed messages. I weeded through the messages one after another, hitting delete at most of them. There were about 20 messages from Dade cursing and screaming. But them there was one from a very mild spoken female. I did not recognize her voice. I wanted to hit delete but listened instead. She requested I call her back so that we could talk. I knew without her saying much. But it was time. I called her back. We made arrangements to have breakfast. Tomorrow at 11am. I'll be there. Panos, on Elmwood.

I woke with the hesitance of winter coming. I made sure to be dressed to impress, even though I was sure she would be thinking the same. I wore a white capri pant suit with a floral print top. I had on a pair of Manolo Blahnik peep toe creations in blush adorned by a floral ornament. They screamed bitch! I grabbed my blush colored clutch and was out the door. I made sure my makeup was on point and my braids were curled hanging free. I wore a pair of hoop diamond cut earrings and the matching bangle. Thank goodness my nails look tight or would have had to stop to have them done before my meeting. I smelled of white jasmine. It was light and not overpowering. I was ready, at least by appearance. I told myself I would be brutally honest. I would be truthful and give her all the pain and hurt she came looking for.

I arrived early. Panos was starting to pick up. I loved eating here there was always something different to try. Plus I loved Greek food. I agreed to be seated at a table and wait for my guest. I made it a point to always be early for important meetings. It was a power ploy and usually showed who had the upper hand. I waited in the upper seating area. I sat there thinking of Sam. I could not wait to see him today. I heard the hostess address someone and said right this way" as they headed up the stairs to my direction.

It was her. She was dressed nice. Not my style but nice. Her makeup was plain. And her hair long but flat. Nothing special.

"Hello" I spoke

Hello" she replied.

"Please have a seat" I added.

The waiter brought over 2 Mimosas.

I broke the silence " So why did you want to meet after all this time? " I questioned."I can only assume that you knew about me all this time and I had no clue you even existed" I concluded. Taking a sip the my drink and holding it in my hands as I sat up and back with the elegance and grace of charm school.

"You're right, I've Known about you for years. I was hoping you were one of his passing fades, that he would come to his senses and leave you but he hasn't" She replied.

The waiter can came to take our orders.

"So now what, we met and go about our lives sharing your husband?" "What do you want from me" I asked demandingly.

"What are your intentions now that you know? Do you love him?" she looked on as her eyes began to swell with water.

"I love Dade. I did not know about you. Even when you showed up at the house, I just assumed you were a random chick he fucked on the side. It wasn't until I saw you with him at the club that it became clear to me that you were anything but random. Them I recalled the many other encounters that that Dade's carelessness placed us in. I'm no angel, but there is something that I need to make perfectly clear to you and your husband, I no longer want Dade. I can not be a part of this fuckery you and he exist in. I love him, but I love me more" I explained.

The waiter brought our food. I ordered the Lamb Souvlaki with a side of Greek Potatoes. Tammy. Dade's wife's name was

Tammy. She ordered the Broiled Haddock With Lemon Pepper. We ate in silence.

Tammy uttered" He loves you. He loves us both. I cry for him. To be torn between two women, two strong women. We have more in common then not"

"You say that as if I should be proud he choose me and you. He vowed to love you. He lies, he cheats and god knows what else. I've watched you cry for him and he return to me in the same breath. There is no pride in that" I argued.

"He loves you. I think more than me. You give him something I can not. I can not fight you anymore. I can not give my husband to you" she spoke calmly.

We ate. Staring at each other.

I knew her pain. The heartache she must be hiding knowing her husband choose someone else. That he loved not just her. That she will never be number one.

I knew that pain. That heartache. I wished we were not alike in this way. We would forever be bonded by Dade's selfish acts. By his love and lies. I would hate him for this. For having me here in this moment. For having to acknowledge his lies.

We finished our lunch.

She left me with these words. "Leave Dade alone and allow him to return to me. He will never leave you, so you must do it. End it now. Let him go"

Little did she know I was already there.

Chapter Thirty-Three

"I Call Your Name"
– Switch

"I Call Your Name"- Switch

Dade

I have been looking for Ayanna everywhere. I'm losing my mind. I needed to explain to her. She doesn't understand. My love for her is real. It's complicated. My love is complicated. I love them both each to a different degree. I married young. I love Tammy. But my heart rings for Ayanna. The passion, the lust, the fire she brings me. I will always be an honorable man. I must make her see, she can love me. I can love her. We can be together. Just as is.

I drove by her house and notice her car has just pulled into the driveway. I see her. I stop the car. She has entered into her home and closed the door. I banged on her door and rang the doorbell.

"Ayanna, let me in" I screamed. "Ayanna, Ayanna!" I continued to call out.

At first there was no answer. I stayed pounding on the door.

"I Know that you're in there I just saw you. We need to talk. I need to talk to you" I commanded.

"Go away Dade, we can talk later" Ayanna yelled back.

"No, Now Ayanna, No now!" I cried

The door opened. Ayanna stood there dressed in a white capri suit. She looked classy and sassy all at the same time. I missed seeing her. She was such a fucking lady. I loved her attitude, especially the one she was given me now.

I walked in. I headed to the living room. She followed closely behind me. We stood there at first silent. Each of us searching for our voice.

"Ayanna, I need to explain somethings to you. The other day at the bar... I.. I. .. The women with me.. She.. I mean She's my.." I took a breath and sighed" Ayanna, the women you saw me with was my wife, her name is.." I was interrupted.

"Tammy, your wife's name is Tammy. I know. I know because I had an interesting conversation with her today. So you are wasting your time Dade" Ayanna blurted out.

"What? When? How long have you known?" I inquired with a puzzled look on my face.

I did not know what to say. There was no lie I could say to justify my deception.

"Dade, All this time we been together. All the plans we had, all the memories we shared and you never thought to tell me you were married." Ayanna spoke as a steady stream of tears rolled down her face. went to hold her, but she backed away from me.

I hated seeing her like this. Anger grew inside of me. How could I have done this, Why would Tammy tell her, Why did Ayanna not tell me she knew?

"Fuck Ayanna!" I screamed. I'm trying to tell you that none of this changes anything. I love you. I want you. There has never been anyone else other than you" I confessed.

"Dade you can't love me, and your wife. You took my choice in the matter away when you lied about being married. We were only playing pretend. You already belonged to someone else. And Fuck I believed that I was the one. The one that could change you. The one you would settle down with, the one you would marry someday. You selfish mutherfucka." Ayanna argued back.

"God Damnit Ayanna!, I want you. Even with all shit you done to me, I want you. We can work through this. Nothing has to change" I'm here calling out for you, can't you see, I love you, I'm in love with you." I said crying out to her.

"Dade I don't know what fuckin world you live in but nothing about me says I'm ok being in 2nd place. Not for you or anyone. You want me, but you have her. You love me and you love her. Your sorry ass can't even make up your mind and chose which one of us you really want. Well I'll chose for you. We're done" Ayanna snapped.

"Bitch, it ain't over till I say it's over. We can work this out. I don't have to chose, I can be with you and her. We've been living like this already. Nothing has to change. You just know now. That is the only difference." I scolded

"Fuck you and your crazy bitch wife! You damn right I know now. And I know I want better, more, something you can't give me. You lied. You kept this secret. Everything about you is a lie! I'm done" Ayanna turned to walk away.

I grabbed her arm and held her.

"You listen to me, I'm not letting you go. You think I'm the only one that lied. You skank bitch, you been fuckin niggas all over town, you think I didn't know. You lied too. You standing here like your sht don't stank. Who you think gonna love you. You think that nigga you was with at the bar gone love you better than me. Uhhh? Don't nobody want you but me. All he want is you pussy than he he gone toss your dumb ass just like the rest. Them what. You come crawling back into my bed. I love you. Nobody else gonna love you, not him not the next." I scolded holding her tight and increasing my grip.

Ayanna was fighting me back trying to escape my grip. I slapped her. She fought back. We were now on the floor wrestling with each other. She kicked and punched. She ran to the kitchen. I ran after her. She grabbed her purse. Opened it and pulled out her .22 and pointed it at me. I stood there.

"Fuck you Dade, Fuck you!" She screamed."I don't need you anymore, Don't come around my place, don't you fuckin call me, when you see me don't even say my name. Me and you are done." she hissed.

"Ayanna, I'm sorry. I didn't mean to hit you. I didn't mean to hurt you!" I pleaded standing with my hands extended out to her. I took a step toward her

We had never fought like this. Usually it was a lot of screaming and yelling, but never physical.

" You take another goddamn step I will fuckin shot" Ayanna vowed. She stood there with the gun cocked. I knew she wasn't playing. I knew she was confident shooting a gun. I just didn't think she would ever be pointing it at me.

"Ayanna LIsten!.. we can work this out.." I protested as I took a step closer to her.

Bang! Went the warming shot.

" I told you not another fuckin step. Get the fuck out Dade. We are done." Ayanna Whispered.

I stormed out of the house. The anger inside of my was boiling over as I wiped the blood from my nose and my eye. That bitch got me good I thought with a sinister grin on my face. Neighbors who heard the gunshot were all outside wondering what was going on. I was not going to let her go. I was not going to just stand there and allow her to walk away. She would pay for this shit. Ayanna belonged to me. I thought as I drove off headed to see Tammy.

I pulled up to the house and stormed in slamming the door behind me. I walked over to Tammy grabbed her and began punching her. One after another I swung on her. I watched as her pretty face became covered in blood. She screamed. She begged me to stop. I couldn't My anger would not allow me to rationalize what I was doing. I hated her for speaking with Ayanna. I hated that I loved both women. I hated that I could not choose. Mostly I hated myself. I sat there beating Tammy until her body lay limp. I snapped out of it I saw what I had done, but it was too late. I cried I begged her for forgiveness. The neighbors must have heard her screams and cries for help. I heard sirens, but I would not run. I needed her to be ok. I needed her to know I loved her and how sorry I was. Please be ok.

"Please be ok Ayanna.. I mean Tammy" I cried as I held her in my arms."I'm so sorry, I'm so sorry"

Chapter Thirty-Four

"Be Mine"
— Miki Howard

"Be Mine" Miki Howard

Anika

I was enjoying myself. After the last time we were at the club, I wasn't sure I wanted to go out for a while. It was almost like old times. Ayanna was the only one missing. I promised her we would catch up soon. I needed to find out more about her new boo and how things were going with her and Dade. We were there with Jay, Que, Mario and here crew. Monica was flashin dough like this bitch was a true baller. I don't know who the hell gave her their black card but she was buying bottles left and right. It was good to see things back to normal. We danced, drank and just had fun. As usual we owned the dance floor. The DJ gave mad shout outs to us. We have VIP on lock. Que and Jay even seemed to be relaxed, sort of. We finished up the last round of drinks and before 3am we were out.

I kissed Monica and Yazz good bye as Jay and Que dabbed laters. Monica pulled off first and then Jay and Yazz. Que, Mario and I rode off. Mario sat in the back seat quiet. Que had some slow jams playing on the car stereo.

He dropped Mario off and watched as he got in the car and headed in the opposite direction. I could only assume to handle business. We drove in silence. This was the first time I had seem Que in weeks. I haven't spoke to him since Ayanna was at my house. I was happy to see that he was ok. I knew with all the drama happening around the city somewhere in there was Que. I was just happy that he was ok. He Drove as Diamond and Pearls by Prince echoed through the car. I noticed that he missed my exit. I assumed he wanted to talk in private so I did not say anything. He looked Damn good. I tried not to stare and played uninterested, but the truth was how could I not. He was that cross between Malik Yoba and Rakim. His complexion was perfect. His voice was smooth and strong. And his walk commanded, demanded respect. He had light brown eyes that told the truth of his reality. As I watched him, his movements were orchestrated. Everything he did was well thought out. From the outfit he wore to the words he spoke. Everything was planned. He was power.

We pulled up to a house located on Lebrun Rd. I wonder who lived here. I had never been to this house and never really drove down this street enough to pay attention to the houses. This was a nice and secluded neighborhood. It was the every edge of the city, not quite in the city and not far enough out to be considered suburban. I had drive pass this street many times and never gave it a second thought. Que parked the car in the back of the house. We got out. He took my hand and I followed him as he lead me to the house.

"Who lives here"I asked. I was admiring the way the home was furnished. It was definitely my style. The color scheme was right, the accent piece were items I would have chosen. Everything about this house appeared to be perfectly plucked from my thoughts.

"I live here. This is where I live" Que uttered.

All this time I had never been to Que's residence. I never even knew where he lived. Guess I never really gave much thought to it. He was always on the go, I guess I never wonder much about this side of him.

"Please make yourself at home" He gestured.

I did. I sat on the loveseat as he lite candles and incense. He had the light in the room on dim. Soon the sweet smell of vanilla filled the room. He poured me a glass of white wine that he just opened. He carried the glass of wine and a double shot of brown liquor with 3 ice cubes over to the love seat. He sat on the coffee table facing me. He gently grabbed my leg and proceeded to remove my Lagerfeld pumps and began rubbing my feet. I smiled sipping my glass of wine.

"I thought it was time you and I talked in private" He spoke calmly. "I think that it is time we speak honestly about us" He continued as he was now working his magic touch on the other foot.

"Que" I paused.

"I already know. Us, I mean We can't ever be... There's too much at stake. Plus I already know I'll never be number one in your life" I commented pulling my leg from his touch.

"Anika, I have loved you since the first day we met. On the playground at Ellicott Creek Park. It was a Sunday July 4th, 1982. You got out of your grandmother's car wearing a red and white star print sundress. You had two ponytails twisted up top and the rest of your hair flowed down your shoulders onto you back. It was curled. You had on a pair of white sandals with a little heel. You had on a gold thin chain with a garnet pendant that hung around your neck.You were the most beautiful girl I had ever seen.I remember asking you cousin who you were. I watched you play with all the other girls. I remember your smile, they way you smelled. I remember when we ran the 3 legged race and you fail down trying to beat me and Boo. You scraped your knee and your grandmother put a strawberry shortcake band aid on it. I recall hitting you with the water balloon. You got made and chased me. I remember thinking that one day me and you would be together" Que confessed.

I sat there listening to him speak. I did not know what to say. I think I heard him say he loved me. I lost my breath trying to avoid his gazing eyes.

"Anika everything I have ever done was and continues to be for us. I know that I haven't always been there when you wanted me too. But I'm here when you need me the most. This house, the money everything is for you. I wanted to make sure that when the time was right, you would never have to worry for anything. That I could be that man you wanted me to be. That I could give you everything you need and want. I will always protect you. I will lay down my life doing so. All I ask is that you be patient Ma. I need you to be patient. You know the type of business I'm in. You know the lifestyle I lead. You know I'm torn. You know there is so much at stake if you and I get together. My first and only thought is to make sure you are ok" He assured.

He had lowered his head. I was staring at a man who was as powerful alone as most third world countries and he had humbled himself to me. My heart raced as he touched my hands. I did not know if I could handle this. I have waited so long to hear him say those things. I too have loved him since the first time I saw him. I knew he was the only man for me. I had waited, waited so long to hear him say those words to me.

"Que why now? Way now? After all this time? After you pushed me away, after you left me so cold hearted, after I cry time and time again for you, You confess this shit to me" I scold as Tears run down my face.

I began to cry uncontrollable. I'm confused. I love this man, but I have feelings for Mr.Cornerback. I was starting to get over him. I was imagining my life outside the streets. Distancing myself from the activities that kept us forever bonded. How could he now. How could he tell me this. I cried

I stood up and walked over to the bay window that faced the from of the house overlooking the dimly lit street light. I felt him hug me from behind. He held me tight. I could not resist him. It was the arms that were to familiar to me. His scent, his heart beat.

I knew them all to well. I cried as he held me. He took my hand and lead me to the master bedroom. It was everything I dreamed for myself. I could see the details they all resembled pieces, items that I had picked out for myself. Things that I had shared in passing with Que. All his time he paid attention. He knew me. He did this, all this for me.

He undressed me button by button. He took his time I was there in my lace shelf bra and matching thong. He looked at me with admiration. Like he finally won his trophy. I was his desire goal. His final victory. He kissed me. My toes, my ankles. He worked his way up my legs reaching my thighs. He was gentle. He was strong and firm, but gentle. He kissed my thighs and worked his way to my core. It was boiling with anticipation. It had been years since we last explored each other. Since I had felt the force of his passion. I lusted after him for years for this very moment. I would not could not hold back. With one finger he pushed the lace covering to the side. He opened my legs and kissed. He kissed each lip as if it was coated in strawberries. He kissed until my strawberry erupted in sweet juice. He tongued his way to the center of my core and allowed every drop of liquid to cascade down his vibrating tongue.

He massaged me with his fingers. He placed one in my pussy and the other on my ass. He gave me his power as he glided his fingers in and out of me. I sat there with my legs wrapped around his neck staring down at him as he loved me. He kissed and stroked, stroked and kiss me as I rocked with his movements. My legs tighten and my back arched. I sang, as tears fell from my eyes. He pulled my closer to him as he plunged deeper and deeper into my universe. It was warm, and wet as eruption after eruption collided with his fingers. I held on to his head as a black hole of ecstasy swell within me. He picked me up. My legs were wrapped still around his neck. His hand rasping my ass. I sat there as he ate and drank from me. Scratching his back and holding on for dear life as he enjoyed me. I cried out in sweet tribal tones. I spoke french, spanish, yoruba, swahili and arabic. I sang hi and low. He drove me mad, as I begged for him to stop torturing me. But he didn't he just continued to control my body. Lick after lick, whisper after whisper he commanded my body. He was in charge of my universal and I was now following his lead. I gave him my soul and he gladly accepted his rank.

He finally released his grip he had on my body. Completing his his mission and accepting his victory. He lay me on the bed and turned me over on my stomach. I lay stretched out as he kissed every inch of my body. From head to toe. He massaged me with his mouth. His breath grazed over my body creating streams of goose bumps everywhere he kissed me. I could feel his body on top of me. Our heartbeats were in sync. He kissed my neck moving my hair from side to side. He pulled me up to him and held me as I sat on his lap. He held me caressing my breast. He kissed me sending me into a daze.

I turned my head to meet his lips so that I could taste my sweet strawberry off his lips. I kissed the juice off his lips, tongue and chin. I licked the remnants off his fingers and enjoy the gift I had given him. I turned around and we kissed. I unzipped his jeans. And slowly began to remove them. I got off the bed and pulled him with me. I untied his boots so that I could remove is pants. His boxers hung heavy from the weight of his dick. I unwrapped Que like a present and slowly began to take him. I wrapped my mouth around his dick. I lotioned it with my spit and caressed him with my tongue. I stroked him up and down as I forced him deep down my throat. He was hard, long and thicker than I recall. I gagged with each motion he made.

I sucked and he moaned, cussed. He played a game of hide and seek with my tonsils as he he moved in and out of my mouth. I sucked him hard and soft. I stroked him with my hands as I teased the tip of his head. He was my scepter. I was his queen and I ruled him with authority. My universe and his kingdom joined in a sacred act of defiance. I went down with the heat of my breath exhaling and came up with the cooling sensation of air from my inhaling. It drove him crazy. I massaged him with the care of twenty nations bowing to me. I sat, prostrated beneath him as he watched me helpless as I commanded his scepter. I whispered grandiose things and promises of a forever after with each stroke of his hard dick. I longed for this moment. It had been years since I enjoyed the thick taste of my heaven. I sat there as he towered over me and I drank all that his scepter provided. I spit it all out as I accepted his seed, I massaged it back onto him and proceeded to suck every drop off of him again and again. He shock with approval as I finished him off to the last drop.

Que grabbed me and sat me on him. I was facing him as I sat on his huge dick. I thought he would need time, but I was sadly and gratefully mistaken. I sat on him bouncing up and down as the scepter now bathed in a sea of gold, It was the King and the Queen, doing battle in a game of chess. I rode him with the pride of evy african queen before me. I wanted to bare this man's children. I saw flashes of a future and the continuance of life with each stroke he gave me. I rode and he thrusted. I arched into him as he sucked on me and scratched my back. I held onto him mad at his untimely confession, yet enjoying his brave honest, truthful words. We stroked and rode each other with the power of 100 horses. Our bodies soaked with sweat as we rode the long journey home. He moved I moved. It was a match not to be won.

He turned me on my back and with my legs in the air pounded me with his thick hard dick. I could see it enter me with force. I could see the my sweet juice cling to his massive rod as he entered and exited me. It was beautiful. He dominated me in a way no man had ever been able to. I loved him for that. I loved my body being able to absorb his power and receive him with such ease. I thanked him over and over again as he stroked my pussy, nailing my sensitive spots with pleasure. I cried out with pain and pleasure. He grunted and went to war for his queen. My legs in the air tied to his hands as he poured into me allowing my juices to drip down his dick with increased excitement.

He turned me over yet again and from behind he entered my innermost circle. It was reserved for only him. I cried out as he forcibly entered me. It took my breath away. I regained get it back as he gently stroked my ass. It was painful and pleasurable at the same time. I could feel the tightness. I could feel him, the veins in his dick.. His heart beating from the excitement and surprise at what we were doing. I enjoyed it. I was lost in our game. Exploring our world and concurring forbidden lands. He loved me, He took me. I gave myself to him willingly. And together we cried out loud in our native tongues.. Enjoying the moment. The pressure I felt was agonizing, but gratifying. He was content loving me this way. He owned his kingdom and his kingship.

He pulled out of me and entered me from behind. He held my waist as he pulled me into him. I bucked back. I shook my ass. He slapped and enjoyed the show. I shook my ass and he slapped and slapped as I bucked back and showed him I could handle that enormous dick. He gave it to me and I took it. It was the queen submitting to her king. I was on all fours as he entered me over and over again. Exploding all over his cock. He screamed with each burst of hot juice that greeted him. I kept presenting gifts of gold singing in my native tongue as he laid nail to hammer and poked my many spots. I came and came as he dived deeper and deeper. I came over and over again as he held me as I rose to ride him. My back was perfectly arched and he held me as I rode him one last time. I rode him on our final quest and together we reached our finish line. We had admitted our true intent. We had given all we could bare. Now let's just hope faite is on board with this new chapter of Que and I.

Chapter Thirty-Five

"What's On Your Mind"
— Eric B & Rakim

"What's On Your MInd"- Eric B & Rakim

Que

I held Anika until the sun rose. She was mine. I would find a way to make this relationship work. I had too. I could not stand another day moment without her here with me. I thought to myself. She was my queen. I wanted her to be the mother of my children. I wanted to see us grow old together. I just needed to make sure this shit happened. I knew she was catching feelings for Ol Boy, but hopefully after last night I have left no question as to my true feeling for her. I'll go to the FAM and ask permission or maybe we'll just do it. Get married. This way they would just have to accept the act. Shit! I'll figure this shit out. I'll make this right, I have too.

Anika lay there peacefully. I hadn't checked my pager at all last night wanted to make sure she had my full attention. Besides I directed everything to Mario. I checked my Pager. There were a few missed calls. I call Jay and checked in. Everything on is end was good. We would meet up later to discuss a few things. I hung up with him and called Mario. He stated he had news. Would meet up with me later to talk. Told him to call Jay and arrange a time. Damn. It's about time. We can finally put this shit to rest. Take out whomever has been fucking with Anika and Yazz. I was already putting a plan into place.

I went back into the bedroom just as sleeping beauty had awaken. Anika was goddamn fine, She was honey caramel complexion. He had curves for days. Her hips swaying from side to side when she walked. And boy was it a sight to see. If was as if she was walking to the beat of a sexy drum pulse. Every nigga I knew wanted to get at her. I remember one day she was having trouble starting the lawn mower and had bent over to check the mower out. It was about 4:30pm when I pulled up. And just in time. Onlookers had been watching her in traffic and she was wearing a pair of daisy duke shorts. Next thing I knew, as I got out of the car was the sound of 4 cars and the Metro bus crashing in front of her house.Scared her half to death and she didn't understand how she could have caused an accident. That just solidified what I already knew, Anika was is a bad bitch, a true dime, eye candy, wife material and one hell of a women. I knew she was always the one. Her hair was permed. She wore extensions from time to time, but her hair was already long. It hung between her shoulder blades right at the middle of her back. It was a dark brown color and It smelled like cupcakes. Her breast were the size of grapefruits. They were full and always perky. I did not understand how her breast stay perky and were so big. Most women I noticed with that kind of breast weight always seem to have back issues or never quite carried them with pride.They were the perfect compliment to her round ass. Anika had a small waist which accentuated her ass and breast. She was shaped like a coke bottle. And each of her assets fit perfectly in my hand.

I stood there admiring her beauty. It was not just surface. She was a beautiful person on the inside. Yeah she could be street, but she was a lady. There was kindness and gentle nature about her, She gave of herself to everyone. She was selfless despite her B-Girl attitude. I loved that she could mingle with the elite of society and then keep it hood for the streets. She was the perfect Bonnie. She laid before me naked. Showing off her curves. Slowly she began to wake. She stretched and walked to the bathroom. Even in the morning she was flawless. She entered the room. She smiled. I loved that I could make that happen.

" Good morning Que" she sang

"Good morning Princess" I smiled back.

"I made breakfast wasn't sure what you wanted so I made pancakes and sausage. I got fruit and coffee, plus cranberry juice. Oh and tea. You wanna join me. She shook head yes and slipped on my t shirt. She was a vision. I took her hand and lead her to the dining room. I had on of my boys find every rose he could find and I dressed the entire front of the house in red roses. There were about 20 dozen red roses scattered throughout the house.

She smiled as she walked over to the them and began to smell them. She turned around to kiss me and I handed her a dozen Calla lilies.

" I know this is your favorite flower, but they are almost out of season. I wanted you to know that I knew." I spoke handing them to her.

She hugged and kissed me."Thank you Que" she cried as tears began to fall from her eye.

I wipe them away.

"Why are you crying" I asked " Did I do something wrong" I added.

"No Que, for once everything seems to be right" she paused. "Everything is just right"

I had her sit down and I severed her breakfast. We ate. I watched her as the many thought went through my mind. I felt lucky. Like I had my lucky charm and no one would ever take it away from me.

" I have something for you" I spoke as her eyes lit up.

"What Que!" she cheered with excitement.

I handed her the first box. It was wrapped in gold wrapping paper and a matching bow.

She opened it like it was her birthday. It was keys to the hose.

"These are your keys to our home. All of this is for you. If there is something you don't like I'll fix it or buy you what you want. If you don't like the house, we can get another one. All I know is that I don't want us to spend another night apart" I vowed.

She looked stunned and was crying. I handed her another box. It was wrapped the same way as the box prior. She opened it. It was keys to the Audi that I had purchased for her. It was candy apple red. She had seen it one day when we were together and I remembered her saying how must she wanted that car in that color.

She hugged me as she ran to the front window and pressing the car remote and admiring the vehicle.

" Can I go see it" she squeaked with joy.

I nodded yes. She took off. I wasn't sure if she remembered she was half naked. My t-shirt just barely covered her ample ass.

But it was too late she was already out the door. I followed. She was already in the driver's seat when I got outside. She looked happy. All I ever wanted was for her to be happy and safe.

"There's one more box" I said as she jumped in my arms and I carried her back into the house before the neighbor could see her nakedness.

I handed her the last box. It was blue. I Could see the excitement in her eyes.

She opened it. There was a platinum garnet and diamond ring size 5 waiting for her.

"This is not an engagement ring, This is a just because ring. I love you and there is no doubt I want you to be mine. My wife and the mother for my children. I'm promising you with this ring that we will be together, That I will take care of you and protect you always. I Love you Ma and I hope you know that." I whispered hoping to make everything I promised come true. She hugged me. She had tears rolling down her face She hugged me and kissed me. My heart skipped. For the very first time I could tell I had made things right between her and I. I was happy. He was happy and I hoped this was the first of many more times I could make her smile.

After breakfast came sex. Anika was hungry for more. I loved her sexual appetite. I had met my match with her. Most girls in my past could not handle my dick. It was either too long, too thick or I was just too much at once for them. Not Anika. Everything about her was different in a good way. Even the way she pleasured me. I was blessed to have her. She was the only person I had ever went down on. The first time I made love to her I knew I wanted her in that way. It was the sweetest favor I had ever had. She tasted that fruit and ice cream and candy. I was instantly addicted to her. I loved the way she tasted and anytime I wanted it, it was now mines for the taking.

We got dressed. I told her I had business to take care off. Gave her some money to enjoy her day. Showed her how to set and disarm the home security system. I made sure she knew how to operate the car phone I had installed. I gave her a kiss and told her I hoped she would be here when I returned. We kissed and I watched her drive off.

I headed in the opposite direction. Business never slept, and I was going to need every single bit of it now. I had to deal with the issue at hand and figure out how to let the FAM know of my intentions with Anika. This day better get easier as the minutes go on. But I knew it wouldn't.

Chapter Thirty-Six

"Wicked"

– Ice Cube

"Wicked"-Ice Cube

Jay

I pulled up to the dungeon just as Mario arrived. We were waiting for Que. Mario was FAM. He was Anika's first cousin. He had been assigned to Que and I to teach him the ropes. At some point Que and I would be taking a more absent role in these streets. Mario was destined to be next in line to run the FAM's empire from the streets. Mario was hard. He didn't say much. He was loyal. He did want we asked and nothing more. He was a quick study. He was gritty. Nothing was too much for him. He was from the Bronx. He mom moved back home after she and his dad divorced. He was a look out kid back in his old hood for the FAM. Yeah The FAM had territories in the city. They were a main supplier to a few Houses scattered throughout the boroughs. I liked this kid. He reminded me of me and Que when we started running Buffalo for the FAM. Girls loved to see Mario coming. He got more ass than any young dude should. And he never had to ask. People knew he was protected. Everywhere we went he got respect. Dudes moved out of is way and honey's watched waiting for their turn. He stood about "5'11. And weighed about 190. I don't judge niggas but by the action he get he must be ok looking. Jay always wore jeans and

Timbs. He had them in every color. He had custom made shits too. If he couldn't find it, he had them made. He told me and Que he had them put steel toe reinforcements at the toes. Said this made stumping niggas that must easier. I was like damn lil nigga you roughless. We laughed.

Que

I pulled into the spot. Jay and Mario were already there. Good I thought. This way we can get to it and I can get home to Anika. I walked in dabbed up Jay and Mario.

I poured us drinks and took my seat at the table. Mario handed out 4 photos.

"The first photo is the bitch that got it out for you. She's Bam's first cousin. She think she knows that we were behind Bam's untimely death. She blames Anika. Figures she get to you Que by hurting Anika. Jay she believes that you also played a role in Bam's death. So the easiest target for you is Yazz." Mario explained.

"So who the fuck is this nigga" Jay questioned pointing at the 2nd picture on the table.

"That's her cousin. He's from Trinidad. He arrived 2 days after Bam went missing. On the island he suppose to be some kind of dope boy. Nothing major. Not affiliated with any major house. Shouldn't be a problem if we take him out. But I'll find out from the FAM. International shit get tricky. Need the FAM to talk to the Shaw Posse of the West Indies to make sure he's not connected." Mario continued.

"So does this mean that Bam is part of an island crew in the city? I questioned.

"No. I thought that too at first, but I did the research. No one claimed him. When we went to the funeral for Bam not one Island crew head was present. But I looked at the family. Connected the dots and nothing lead back to anyone here. He was a lone soldier, small time." Mario confessed. "However, chicky from Down

South, I wanted to see what we could bring up on her, but I got no response from the FAM in NC. Weird right?" Mario continued.

"So what does this have to do with the other 2 people in the in the photo." I asked.

"Well this bitch Tonya was one of Bam's boys old lady. Yeah he was hanging out with the girls and went down in the crossfire. She got it out bad for each of yall. She thinks that Yaz was JR's type and believes she's the reason he was killed. We know it ain't true, but a bitch gonna think what she want." Mario concluded.

"Let me guess, this mutherfucka think he gonna avenge Bam's death by fucking with us" Jay laughed.

I laughed too. "So what we looking at Mario, what's the damage and how soon can we react?" I inquired.

"I just need to present this information to the FAM and I should know by the end of the week if not sooner. Mario confirmed.

"Good, I need this shit to be done. It took us long enough to put this shit together. I want it done before some more shit pop off" I spoke

Jay shook his head in agreeance and so did Mario.

We finished our drinks and we each went back to our lives.

Chapter Thirty-Seven

"Right Here"

– SWV

"Right Here"- SWV

Ayanna

What a hell of a week. I had to call the police and get an order of protection against Dade. After I heard what he did to Tammy I just could not take any chances. I heard they had him in county until he makes bail. That could be any day now.I sent flowers to Tammy as she was recovering at Buffalo General Hospital. I didn't hate the bitch. I just hated what Dade had put us through.

I had taken a few vacation days to get myself together. I was spending more time with Sam. was excited about my future even if it wasn't with him. I now had a clearer path to what it was I wanted and who I wanted to spend it with. I had meet the girls for dinner and explained everything that went down between me and Dade. We laughed at me pulling the gun on that crazy mutherfucka. It was so good to have everyone present. I had missed my girls and partyin like crazy. On the low, I was thinking about calming my ass down a touch. I was trying to work on me and get my shit together. I hadn't told anyone but Anika. She gave me her full support. It seemed like this summer was full of surprises for everyone. Yazz and Jay were getting even more serious. Anika had told us about her dilemma between Que and Mr. Cornerback. I told her to just follow her heart and don't regret it. Monica was the only one still wildin` out. But even she was taking a more back seat approach as summer neared its end. It just felt like old times.

Sam had picked me up. We were spending more time together and I loved every minute of it. I was practically living him. I would go to my place to check things out. By I was thinking about renting it out and moving in with him. It was his suggestion. I keep thinking about it. I had taken the braids out and had my hair permed and weaved to perfection. It was blown straight and hung down my back. Sam loved it. I loved the way he looked at me. He made me feel like a queen. He was a gentlemen all the time. We talked all the time sometime for hours in the bed, in the car when we weren't together anywhere about everything. It was refreshing. And yet we still had not had sex.

I watched him as he drove. He listened to Jazz. Jazz. He was smooth and calm. He and Dade were like night and day. Sam was so mellow. We drove to the movie Theater at the Thruway Mall. It was packed. I was looking forward to watching Aliens 3. I was a big sci-fi fan and closing out the trilogy was a must. Sam was not into sci-fi but I managed to catch him up on the action by watching the first 2 movies on the VCR. I did not care really about the movie I just wanted to spend time with Sam.

We finished the movie and on to dinner. I took him to one of my favorite spots. Mulligans was a french bistro restaurant on Hertel not too far from the old Sibley's store. It was romantic. I managed to show Sam my cultured side. I allowed myself to be vulnerable. No walls,no layers, no bridges, just me being transparent. He saw me. He understood me without judgement and he was still here, in this restaurant enjoying himself, with me. For the first time in a long time I did not want to be anyone else but me Ayanna Nicole Freeman. Just a girl with dreams and a new definition of the word love. I was ready.

We arrived at Sam's place. What a wonderful day. I was able to be carefree and let my hair down and breath. It felt good and so did Sam. He held me as we danced as "Lose Control" by Silk played in the background. I felt things I had not allowed myself to feel in years. This man was everything.

"Whatever it is you desire" he whispered along with the song "Lick you girl from left to right" he continued.

He had me. I was ready for love. I was ready for Sam. It was time, I wanted to thanked him for being the man every girl deserves. I was happy he waited for me and tonight I would show him just how thankful I could be. The song played on repeat and we were lost in the harmonious tunes. The perfect harmonies of the the song. It was beautiful. He kissed me and I kissed him back. He slipped my dress off of me as I unbuttoned his shirt. We continued to dance not missing a step with the beat. I stood their in my bra and panties and he in his boxers. Held me. My body pressed into his naked chest. He was warm. His touch so gentle. My body ached, longed for him. My insides cried for the inevitable introduction of him and me. It was time. He unsnapped my bra as I removed his boxers. They fell simultaneously to the floor. He removed my panites with his teeth. Pulling me to the floor with him.

As the echoes of Silk played "Whatever it is you desire

I want to give my baby

I want to feel your body yearn

All your softest spots I want to learn

Baby won't you let me just kiss you down

Make you spin around and 'round

Flip you girl from left to right

If you don't mind

Baby can I just spend the night"

Sam asked and I whispered yessss.

We made love right there. I gave and he received. He gave and I loved every bit of this magical moment. It was beautiful. iT was everything Love was meant to be.

One man and one women loving each other. I cried on the inside. It was what I 've always wanted. How I had always believed it should be. I had fooled myself into accepting the falsehood of what others had given me. But no more. I was worthy. I was capable and Sam was showing me the way. We made love. We made sweet love over and over as if we were on repeat and Silk's Lose Control was our anthem.

"Can I turn you on

Can I turn you on

Till the break of dawn baby"

Yess, yess, yess I answered as the music played on.

Chapter Thirty-Eight

"My Minds Playing Tricks On Me"
– Geto Boys

"My MInds Playin Tricks on Me"- Ghetto Boyz

Dade

Damn! I can't believe they had me locked up for 4 days. I tried calling Ayanna have her come and get me out, but I couldn't get a hold of her. My boyz told me they let Tammy out the hospital. Said I did a number on her. I wasn't feeling good about what I had done to her. My first stop would e to checkon Tammy. I needed to apologize. I needed to make things right. I stopped off at the flower shop. I purchased a few dozen flowers. I wasn't sure if she would see me, but hell I was going home. At some point sTammy was gonna have to deal with me. I just hoped that we could come to a point where she forgives me and understands me and Ayanna's relationship.

I walk into the house. Tammy's cousin Marco was sitting in the front room. He was here visiting from Trinidad. Tammy was lying propped up on the couch. Her face was still bandaged. She appeared to have her ribs wrapped too. She just looked at me. I could see the pain in her eyes. Toya was by her side. As usual. THose two were as thick as thieves. They had been best friends since childhood. Ever since Tammy moved to the states when she was 5, her first friend she met was Toya. They lived next door to each other in Langfield. Both of them gave me a fuck you look. BUt I did not care. I was home and I was going to see my wife.

I walked over to her. Kissed her hand as she looked the other was. I handed her the flowers I had purchased. I kneeled right there at her side and rested my head in her lap. I cried and begged for her forgiveness. I told her I would never raise my hand to her again. I told her I was not sure what came over me. I told her I loved her. I was ashamed at what I had done. I begged and pleaded until I felt her run her fingers through my twist. I had missed her touch. I knew she loved me. She had forgiven me. It would take time for her physical scars to heal, but her heart was already willing to overlook my flaws. Resting in her lap, I knew everything would be right. That she would one day accept me, and my love for Ayanna too.

I changed my clothes and got dressed. I could hear Toya downstairs cussing me out. I could hear her telling Tammy she needed to leave me. I just smiled. Tammy loved me and was too loyal to our marriage to ever just walk away. Besides she knew that I loved her. "She couldn't and wouldn't" I thought confidently. I was feeling cleansed after my 4 day stay in County. I had things to take care of and people to see. I walked down stairs and whispered to Tammy that I would be back later. She looked at me and whispered "Don't Go, Stay" IT was the first time I had noticed that her mouth was wired shut. Damn.

"I need to go handle business women. I'll be back" I commented

I could see Toya glaring at me. I smiled and told her I loved her. I would return but right now I needed to see Ayanna. I needed to make things right with her too.

I pulled up to Ayanna's I got out and walked up to the door. I rang the doorbell and banged on the door. I tried y key, but she had changed the locks. I waited in the car for about 20 minutes to see if she would come home. I was just about to leave when a Blue Audi pulled up in the DRiveway. A nigga got out and then opened the passenger door and out stepped Ayanna. What the fuck. I jumped out of the car and walked upto the both of hem.

I could tell by the look on ayanna's face she was shocked.

' Dade, I know you know I have an order of protection out against you. You need to leave' she stated

I don't give a fuck about no order. Who da fuck is dis" I demanded.

"Dade you need to go" Ayanna replied as she opened the door " I'm calling the police"

The nigga looked at me as if he wanted some.

"Nigga, you know who I am? You know what I can do to you for fuckin wit my girl?' I questioned.

He stood there looking at me. He grabbed Ayanna and walked into the house behind her. Ayanna slammed the door. I banged on the door behind them.

"Ayanna open dis fuckin door" I cried

"Go away Dade. the police are on their way" she replied.

"Fuck dat! We need to talk now"

I heard the door lock.

I heard the sirens of police cars approaching. I got back in my car and drove away.

Fuck that shit. Dat Bitch is going to talk to me. She needs to understand that She's mine. I love her. If I can't have her no one will" I yelled. That was that nigga from the bar that night, I thought. Who the fuck was he. Where did he come from. I would find out. I will put an end to this shit.

Chapter Thirty-Nine

"Keep On Movin"
— Soul II Soul

" Keep on Movin" - Soul II Soul

Yazz

I woke up in a cold sweat. I hated having nightmares. It's been awhile since I had one, but the one I just had brought it all back. My great grandmother believed that the spirits talked to us through our dreams. That they left hidden messages or gave warnings of what was to come. When I was little I remember her telling me that I had the gift. I never knew what she was talking about, but I did not want it whatever the gift was. She said that one day I would understand, if I stopped fighting it and just accepted the gift. With every nightmare and dreams I had I could relive it vividly the next day. I would tell my great grandmother all about with the burden, them and she would share her wisdom with me. For the most part they were pretty fun and nothing serious. Until one night my dream to a horrible turn. I remember waking up in tears and screaming at the top of my lungs. My great grandmother tried to get me to talk about it, but I couldn't and wouldn't. That was the last time that chose to believe in anything I dreamt of or understand their meanings. But the dream I've been having, this new nightmare was repetitive. I have been having this dream for the last 2 weeks. Night after night it hunts me. It is full of death, sadness and blank faces crying. I can feel the fear, and the lose of love. The dream is cold. The pain and grief is so real. The heartache is strong and at the end of the chaos that happens is me. I am in the center of it. Every night the intensity of the dream tightens and the dream becomes more clear, the faces, the events and the emotions, they are all stronger. I've tried not to see it. I cry because I know it is more that just a dream. I don't want to pay attention to the callings of spirits, but are telling me,and my heart is heavy. I cry every night and wake every morning with tears and the burden that something bad is coming our way. I pray that I am not right, but like before when I was young, I hated my dreams because they were always right.

I told Jay about my dreams and he tried to assure me that everything was going to be ok. He would tell me that nothing was going to happen to anyone, not me , you, Anika, Que, Monica or Ayanna. I tried to tell him about what saw and he tells me not to put more stock into it than what it is , a dream. I smile and pretend that everything is ok. I dare not tell Monica's ass she gone think I've been smoking that good junga! Maybe what I need is to have a girls day. To see everyone . This will put me at ease, I hope. A little bit of normalcy is what I need to blow these blues away. I call up the girls and plan a night out. It was party time and maybe shaking my ass on the dance floor would be enough to shake this feeling.

It was a fun night out. More important it was drama free. We drank, smoked and danced. The Squeeze Was packed as usual. There were only so many places to go the the b-lo and tonight it looked like everyone showed up here. There are always a few songs that get the party started and get everyone ass on the dance floor. So when the DJ played "It Takes 2 " by Rob Base and DJ EZ Rock.we all got up and went on the dance floor and stayed there. Anika and I were dancing on the speakers, while Monica and Ayanna were on the dance floor. Song after song the DJ was jamming. We were all looking fly as usual and had acquired onlookers and admirers as we danced. BUt this time other than Monica everyone just smiled and enjoyed the attention. There was no hooking up, taking of numbers or unnecessary flirtation. It was different. Up until now that's what we were about, looking good, flirtin' with niggas, partyin' and getting that money. We were the original party girls.we lived up to our titles. Every girl wanted to be us and every dude wanted to know us. We drank, smoked and just had pure fun. But something had changed. We had changed. And we might be time to hand our titles down to the next crop of girls to carry on the legacy.

Chapter Forty

"Time 4 Sum Aksion"
— RedMan

"Time 4 Sum Aksion"- RedMan

Jay

According to Mario we were ready to move. He managed to to get more intel on the marks, There was definitely a closer connect them we thought. It could lead to a serious issue, but the FAM said to go ahead and take them out. And once the command is given our job is just to make sure we carry it out. Besides I can only keep Yazz locked up for so long. She was starting to get restless. I was just try to protect her, but I can see that this situation and the lifestyle is taking a toll on her. I can't ask her to give up any more of herself for me. I'm just relieved that this will all be behind us soon and we can get back to some regular shit.

Que

Mario had told us the missing links to the shitheads that were after Anika and Yazz. It seems there may have been a another connection to their crew. I'm having Jay and Marion meet me at the spot.we need to go over the plan. It's about time this shit is put to rest. After this I can finally move on with Anika. I had gotten the blessing from the family to be with Anika. In fact they were happy about us being together. I wanted to how her how serious I was about being there for her and my love. I had purchased a ring. Damn there dropped 20 g's on that fucker. I recall her saying how she loved pear shaped diamonds. What I didn't know was that them shits was rare as fuck. So I had the jeweler find me one a big one. He came back with a 5ct pear shaped diamond. I then had to customize the setting and band because the shit was so big. BUt it would be worth it just to see the look on my Anika's face. I wanted her to know how much she meant to me and that I would spoil her and give her everything her heart wanted. Damn I loved that girl and soon the the whole world would know.

Monica

I got the call from Mario to meet them at the spot. After that last job i did for them, I thought some easy cash would be nice. I pusshed up n some nigga Que and jay had been looking for. I had been spending a little time with him. HIs dumb ass really think I'm into him. He and his friend came thru last night. I got them high and them these punk mutherfuckas want to start yapping their mouths. I figure I better let Que, Jay and Mario handle this shit. Although I wanted to blast their asses for what they have been doing. I'm sure once I fill the Que in on this it would be a matter of time. And good, because I gave up some good dick fucking around with these wanna be gangstas.

Que

I pulled up to the dungeon. Mario and Jay were already there. MOnica had pulled up behind me. We walked in together. This bitch was nasty. I looked at her as if she was a dude. She had balls and wasn't afraid to get grimmy. We used Monica from time to time because she could get close to our enemies and they were none the wiser. I almost fucked with Monica. She wasn't back looking. In Fact she was stacked. She had body for days and she had a pretty face. She was street and sassy. Dudes everywhere were always trying to get at her. But she was deadly. She came with too much drama. DRama that could get a nigga killed. And to top it off she could careless. She used men, like some dudes used women. Them she would toss you to the curb like you were trash. She was a bad bitch. Anyone going up against her better be ready to take her ass out because she knew too much and if the price was right she would talk. Her only saving grace was that she was damn there family to Anika. And had become an asset to the FAM. Other then that Monica was toxic. And I was happy I dodged that bullet.

We were all seated inside. I hd poured drinks and we listened as Monica talked. I was right the connection was closer than we thought. Monica told us that the Trini dude was here to assist his cousin kill the dudes that killed their cousin Bam. She was targeting their girlfriends and had plan to take them out too. There were going to move on them the other night at the Squeeze but they had a last minute change of plans. The other guy was a family friend and he was here to help out. He mentioned that he had connections to the Shaw Family. But we knew that could not be true based on the conversation that the FAM conducted with the Shaw's. So this mutherfucka was laying. This was either a serious red flag cause this nigga was an imposter which usually meant he was Fed or he was just trying to big up his rep. Either way we were given the go so it was on.

Monica continued to tell us what she knew. We paid her for her services and let her go.

Wow. We needed to contain this shit. I allowed Anika to go out with me but I did send some soldiers to the Squeeze to make sure she and the girls were ok. I told Jay we could just sit back and give them some space, but we needed to protect them, so we sent soldiers in that they did not know. This way if something went down the girls had backup. Me and Jay were outside in the parking lot anyway just in case.

We went over the plan. This shit comes to an end tomorrow.

Mario called in the crew and let everyone know the plan. Jay and I listened. Mario was ready to lead. Jay and I had taught him everything we knew. He had power and respect in the streets. It was time and I'm sure that after this hit the FAM would agree. It was time for Mario to take over and have me and Jay do something us. Besides we ran these streets for the past 10 years, it was time to pass the torch and who better to take over than Mario. This just might be good timing too. I wanted o be able o plan my future with Anika and I know Jay wants to do right by Yazz. That nigga might even want out period. I can only speak for myself, but i stacked enough money up to retire good if I had to. I even have a few investment properties here and there, so I was good. I knew Jay was smarter than the average nigga, so my dude should be pretty set if he chose to walk.

I mean he and Yazz would be ok. I had never been excited about finishing a job but this one was a life changer.

Chapter Forty-One

"When My Homies Call"

– 2Pac

"When My Homies Call" Tupac

Monica

Knowing what I know I thought it was best to keep an eye on my girls. I had made plans to hang out with Marco. I was suppose to meet him at his cousin's house for a get together. This should be interesting. But in the meantime I was going to hang out with Ayanna and Anika. And Yazz. We were planning a Spa Day. Que had set this up for us. This way we would be out of the way while things went down.I had learned to not ask questions, I was being paid to do a job. So if this is what Que wanted I was happy to cash that check. Besides it would be good for me to see my girls. I was so busy getting niggas money that I haven't been hanging around them much.

I was meeting Yazz and Anika at Ayanna's. When I arrived at her crib, Sam was there. It was cool, because I did not really have a chance to get to know him. He seem mad cool. Much different than Dade's crazy island ass. Ayanna seemed so at peace with Sam. The way they looked at each other, the way he talked to her, watched her I could tell he caught feeling for her. It was cute and sicken watching them interact. But I was happy for her. Hell I was happy for all my bitches. If you want one nigga one dick, than have at it. That shit was just not for me. At least not right now. The thought alone made me want to smoke a blunt.

BUt truth, I was happy for Ayanna. IT was time she found a real man who would love her without the drama.

"Alright enough of this lovie dovie shit" I yelled smiling at Sam"Yall gonna make me throw the fuck up" I laughed.

"Don't be mad cause I got some new dick that's mine" Ayanna clapped back.

"Oh so is that all I'm good for Ayanna" Sam chimed in

"Boy please. Dick and money all a hoe know" Yazz laughed.

" Stop giving Sammy such as hard time " Anika teased Yall know he the only man here. We might need him to change the light bulb or some shit" She laughed.

Sam just sat there and laughed. He took the teasing like a champ. It was cute. I could tell he was a good dude. I could tell that he would be around for a while.

It felt like old times. It was just as it should be me and my girls hangin and mackin.

Yazz

These girls are crazy! Monica was clowning Sam. We were all laughing and having fun. It felt good to be out of the house. More importantly I was with my girls. I knew things were changing. Just as summer was coming to a close, so was this phase of our lives. The original around the way girls had found love and were no longer standing at the bus stop suckin on a lollipop. We were still go gettas, we were still fly but we were maturing

It was cute to see us all cuddled up with our dudes. I had faith that someday MOnica would find her prince, but know her ass it would be a king, cause that bitch need someone who owns the fuckin kingdom let alone got the money to back it up. BUt sure as shit her day was coming. For now it just felt right. All of us laughing and acting silly made me forget all about my nightmares. Made me relax and just enjoy today.

Anika

Look at us. I sat there with the camera taking pictures. WE had been thick as thieves for as long as I could remember. We were sisters. Today was just another day to add to the memories. I was happy for Yazz and Jay. I hoped they would end up married one day. They were so cute and happy together. And now Ayanna and Sam. I was impressed. Sam was everything I had hope for my girl. And the fact that he sat here in the lioness den and took the torture showed he could hang. Ayanna smiled the whole time. It was like he brought the sunshine to her world. Hell he cheesed just as hard as she did. They were in love and we all could see it. I was happy. Que was happy. And all was good. Monica was Monica, but there was no changing her. And that's what I loved about her.

Her free spirit and wild side. It brought out the fun in all of us. Our friendship was solid These were the stories that I could see us sharing with our kids when we were older. Telling them about how we use to shake our asses, flirt and cause all kinds of trouble.

I took a few more shots with the camera.

"Girl if you don't put that damn camera down" Monica yelled.

"Shut up, I'm tryna capture yo raggedy ass s people know what you look like without all yo shit on" I laughed back at her.

"Bitch you better not" Monica replied. "Or I'll show Que that picture of you when had a Jheri curl fro!!" She laughed.

We all laughed even Sam.

"I know you ain't laughing Sam you just wait til we get some shit on you" I warned

It was good times.

Ayanna

"Yall gonna leave my man alone" I laughed

"Oh so now he ya man. You get a little dick and you claimin him" Monica joked

"Shut up!" I laughed spitting my pop out and it sprayed out all over the floor.

We all busted out in full laughter. You would have thought that we were drinking something other than Tahitian Treat or Nehi Peach pop. I loved these times that we were together. MOnica and her goofy ass, with Yazz and Anika just being silly. I loved the way Sam just held his ground. It was good to see him interacting with my peeps. It mattered to me that they liked him. It was cool for him to see me in my element. JUst me and my girl wildin out.

They had jokes for days. It was funny as hell. We laughed and joked and drank our pop. Not every day or memory is of us clubbin and freaking niggas on the dance floor. It was times like this that meant the most. Just us having fun. These are my girls, my sister for life and nothing could ever change that.

Monica

"Yo hoes it's time to get gone. We gonna be late for our Spa Day if we don't get out of here." I announced. I finished my sip of pop and went to check my hair in the mirror in the front room.

I had noticed that a familiar car just pulled up in the driveway. I just know this nigga ain't just showing up I thought.

"Aye Ayanna, Ummm. WE got company. Dade just pulled up you want me to get rid of this nigga" I said clappin my hands like I was ready for some action.

" No. I got this" Ayanna answered.

Ayanna walked to the door and her herd of lioness were right behind her.

"Dade didn't I tell you not to come back around here," she spoke calmly.

We all looked at him like try something nigga. Sam stood there. We all had her back. It was time this ningga got thee point.

Chapter Forty-Two

"Sometimes I Rhyme Slow"
Nice N Smooth

"Sometimes I Rhyme Slow" Nice & Smooth

Dade

I just want to talk to you. No harm in that. Just talk... Alone. Outside.Please!" Dade begged as he looked at us.

Ayanna said it was ok.I heard her ask her crew to clean up and grab her purse and lock up the house she would meet us outside.

She walked outside. We were sitting on her front porch. I just wanted to tell her how sorry I was. I wanted to let her know how much I loved her. I did not want to scream and cuss. I just wanted her to know that we could make this work. I would try real hard to watch my temper. But to see that nigga in the house with them told me I might be too late. I was loosing my love. I could not lose her.

Ayanna, girl, I love you, I need you. Please don't do this. I need you. We could make this work" I pleaded.

"Dade we can't. I need you to let me go. I just can't be with you anymore. If you love me let me go. Go home to your wife. We just can't and I won't. Please respect my decision." she said getting up.

I saw her walk away i went to reach for her, but I just couldn't I screamed

"I love you gayl, I love you and only you forever"

She turned around and gave me a smile. I knew she heard me. I knew she knew i cared for her.

What I didn't notice was Tammy's car pull up. She had gotten out of the car and was standing right there. She had heard me confess my love for Ayanna. She knew I would never love her the way my heart beats for Ayanna. I loved dem both, but I loved Ayanna More. She heard me and I could not take it back.

Ayanna

I knew Dade loved me but it was poisonous. Our relationship was not healthy. It was based on manipulation, lies and fear. I was no longer that girl. I had out grown whomever he was in love with. I Was no longer that girl. I knew he knew that. I know that he knew this was the last time we would be here in this moment. What we shared was fun and sad at the same time. It was filled with memories of pain. I did not crying then I did laughing. The sex was good, but that can't be all there is to us. I was done. I walked away. I smiled at him, and started to head back towards the driveway. I heard Monica's big mouth and Everyone laughin. I saw Sam. He smiled at me and I knew everything would be ok. I walked toward them it was time to get our Spa day started.

Dade is over and I'm starting a new chapter to my life. First Chapter Happiness.

I was almost the the group when I heard a strange, but familiar sound it was close and before I could turn around..........

BANG….. BANG….BANG...BANG!!!!!!- Shots were fired.

Chapter
Forty-Three

"How I Could Just Kill A Man"
— Cypress Hill

"How I Could Just Kill A Man" -Cypress HIll

Que

Intel told us that everyone we was looking into was at the address that Monica gave us. There was 2 males in the house. The 2 girls had left. THey seemed to leave in a hurry. I gave the word and Mario and his crew moved in on the house. It was broad daylight and we were handling business. We had the block covered. Eyes everywhere. Mario went in from the back door and 2 went in the front door. Never leave the screen door unlocked.

It was easy access. That told me that they had no Idea who they were fuckin with.

The caught them off guard. One shot two shot. The rest was just showing off. They pooped 10 bullets into each of them. Just for the hell of it. They turned up the music and was in and out before anyone noticed a thing. It was summer so it would be a while before someone noticed that the smell of wood burning was not barbeque but the burning house.

Jay

My pager was going off like crazy. I needed to get to the phone. I have a bad feeling about this. Mario paged me with the all clear code. But then I received another code from him.

I pulled over and called Mario.

"What the fuck"

I 'm headed in the direction of Ayanna's house. I pass Que. I see him and we make eye contact. He follows suit by doing a nast"Uy"n the middle of a busy street. We head down Fillmore when I spot the bitch we after. I make a nasty turn to follow her.

Both them bitches are in the car together. THey make right and then a left headed toward the highway. Que watching me knows exactly what I was thinking.. We break. I follow closely behind their car. We enter the intersection at Deerfield and Litchfield I follow them.I know exactly where they are going I page Que, bu I know he is one step ahead of me.

Que

What the fuck. My pager is going off. I can't stop now. tHe look in Jay's eyes told me we needed to handle this shit and get these bitches. Whatever the issue is it has something to do with them. When I get my hands on this bitch. She is dead.. I spot Jay's car. I'm looking for a cut across. I know exactly where she is headed. Dumb bitched had no idea that we did our fuckin homework, plus Monica gave us the address. She exists at the Suffolk exit. She pulls up to the light. Jay pull sup on the side of her car, just as I Pull up at the light. I have the green light so I block her car. I could see her and the other chick talking. Jay looked and we both exited our cars. Before they could even know what happened, Jay had let on shot to the passenger's head and I shot right there the front window. Tammy and Toya were dead. Gunned down just like their punk as niggas and her bitch ass cousin. Jay let into them and so did I . It was the perfect ending to a bitch that had stepped out of her lane. She was don and so was her wack as crew.. The car sat there at the light as the light turned green with the horn bleepin from the heavy weight of Tammy's slumped body pressing against it. We were out.

Chapter
Forty-Four

"They Reminisce Over You"
Pete Rock &CL Smooth

"They Reminisce Over You" -Pete Rock & CL Smooth

Que

I drove as fast as I could. I arrived at the hospital.i parked at the emergency exit. I'm sure I was parked illegally, but I could careless about a ticket right now. I just needed to get there. "I should've been there", I scold myself. Every bad thought imaginable was racing through my mind. Please let her be ok. Please, I begged.I just can't. I did not stop at the emergency desk, I just started yelling for Anika, "Anika!!", "Anika!! I yelled wandering through the ins and outs of the emergency area. The older lady at the help desk came over to calm me down.

"Get the fuck off me!, where is she!" I barked scaring the older lady half to death.

" Right here Que"I heard the faint sounds of Anika's voice. She had been crying. Her eyes were red and puffy. I ran to her and wrapped my arms around her. I held her tight as she cried uncontrollably I noticed that Monica was who was normally talkin shit at a loss for words, as she cried a steady stream of tears. Monica and Yazz were consoling each other. Where was Ayanna, where was she?

"Anika .. Ayanna what happen, where is she?' I questioned, knowing i would not like the answer.

"She's …. " Anika could not even finish her sentence. .

"Fuck!!!" I screamed.

I kissed Anika's head and held her. I just held herr as she cried.

I noticed there was a dude there with the girls. It had not dawned on me that Ayanna's new man was there. Damn That fucked up. He saw her get shot. He was sitting in the chair with his head held low and his hands were covering his face.

I loosened my hold on Anika. I walked over to him. And just rested my hand on his shoulder. I could imagine what he was going through. I would lose my mind if this had been Anika. I also knew what it was like to lose someone close to you.

Hell I knew what it was like to take a life and yet, being on the other side of the equation was no easier than pulling the trigger. He just shook with grief. There were no words I could say or anything I could do. If this man loved Ayanna even half as much as I loved Anika, then there was nothing that would console him other than bringing Ayanna back. I did not even know him. BUt I knew his pain. And there was nothing to take that away.

Monica

Shit!! I can't believe she's gone. We were just joking and laughing. I can't believe that bitch shot Ayanna. I cried. I cried like a baby. We were sisters. And it felt like I had lost a piece of me. My heart ached. All I could do was replay the horrible scene over and over again. I want it to stop, but it won't. I can't stop crying. I can't stop hurting. I hope that fuckin bitch get what she has coming to her.

Tear rolled down my face as I relive the the thought that my sister is gone. I can't believe she is gone.

Jay

"Over here" I heard Que call me in their direction. Damn it , Goddamnit. I could not believe this shit happened. My eyes were searching for Yazz. All I saw was sadness, Monica, Anika and Yazz. Everyone was crying. I rushed to Yazz's side and held her. I wish i could take the pain away. I wish that I could have gotten to that bitch Tammy sooner. I wished… I wished Ayanna was here. Just the thought was absurd, the 4 musketeers, they were inseparable.It was always Anika, Ayanna, Monica and Yazz. This just isn't making any sense. None of this is making any Fuckin sense. I held Yazz and Monica and allowed them each a shoulder to cry on. They cried and with each tear I thought about Tammy and Toya and how each bullet we loaded into them still did not measure upto the one bullet that she shot into Ayanna.

The doctor came out. He asked if we were able to contact her family. Anika said that her mother and Father were on their way. He told us that Dade was in serious condition. tHe bullet just missed his heart and lung. He would more than likely have to walk with a cane, but the surgery went well. They were moving him down to intensive care. The doctor asked if we had notified his family. We all remained silent.

How fucked up. Dade loving 2 women and now both of them dead. What a fucked up situation. What a shity ass way to wake up, knowing that you wife killed the one person you truly loved. KNowing that he played a role in not having either one of them to cry over him. I know that asshole would be heartbroken knowing Ayanna was gone. I'm not sure he's going to be ok after this one. Dade may have been on crazy ass dude, but I know one thing for sure he loved him some Ayanna. It was crazy love but love nonetheless. BUt fuck him and his wife. Th only one that matters is Ayanna.

Yazz

I can't, I can't" I cried. "Ayanna!! Ayannnna!" my voice screamed out in pain. I was covered in her blood. I see her laying there in the grass I see her lifeless body fall. I hold her. Screaming." I can't, I can't" I cried. She was my friend, sister, ace and partner in crime. How could this happen. Why did that bitch shoot her. My heart. I could not catch my breath. The pain was too much. The pain was too much. All I could do was cry. Cry and recall the friend that was gone. What I held in my hands was not the was not Ayanna. Ayanna was playful, full of life, fun loving, cheerful, loving and brave person. She took that. That she took that away. "I just can't, I can't" I cried.

I just rested my head on Jay's shoulder and wished all this a dream. I wished, i had not foreseen these events, I wished for just once my dreams were wrong, That this pain would turn and go away, that Ayanna was still standing, that we were getting or nails done. That my thoughts were just figments of my imagination, and not thoughts put into actions. Damnit!! I knew, up I can't. I can't accept that this is it. I want my sister back, how about I dream about that . I'll dream about her, and bring her back.I'll pray that dream comes true.

Anika

I had tried to explain to Ayanna's parents what happen. I tried to fight the tears but, my heartfelt pain got the best of me.

Ayanna's mom just cried uncontrollably. Her father a usually proud and statued man was brought to his knees. The doctor took them back to see her.

They held each other. There was no amount of money, nor status that they could achieve that would have repared them for this moment. It was unfair that they had been placed in this situation. It was not easier for for me to accept this as my new reality, but Ayanna was their love of their life. Their Pride and joy. And now she was no more. I cried. I cried for their lose. I cried at my lose. I cried at this fucked up situation. I just cried because the pain was too great to bare. My sister, my friend was gone.

I heard the a familiar voice. I could not make out the conversation, but I certainly recognized the voice. I looked up just in time for Mr. Cornerback to lock eyes with me as he stood at the ER service desk. He ran to me. I could not hold back. He held me and I cried. Not even thinking of Que. I allowed those now familiar hands to hold me as I tried to gain my composure but failed. I felt secure and safe. I als knew I was torn. It had been a few days since I had an opportunity to talk with him. Things had moved so quickly with Que that I never had a chance to break things off with Mr. Cornerback. I was so happy that he was here, but I did not know how he knew. How did he know I was here, That I needed him.

He looked down at me and wiped tears from my eyes. He told me that he had recognized the house on the news and new that I would be here. He hoped that I was not injured. He hoped that me and my friends were safe. But the news report gave a gray outcome. So he came to make sure I , we were ok.

He kissed my forehead and held me. I thanked him for his support, but told him that I really needed to be here for my friends right now. That I loved him for running to my rescue, but right now I needed to focus on Ayanna's family. I told him I would call him later when I got home. THat we would talk them. We kissed and he said his condolences to Monica, and Yazz. He noticed Que and Jay and acknowledged them with as simple nod. He walked over to Sam as they have met on several occasions and comforted him. We hugged when he was done and he left.

I could feel Que's eyes on me. He had watched another man show the same concern for me as he had. I knew that Que was aware of my feeling for Mr.Cornerback.And Now, he knew he loved me too. He did not say anything, but his facial expression said it. And with the shit Ayanna just went through fighting through a love triangle was the least of my worries. I had made my decision so there was no need worry.

We hung around the hospital. Que and Jay needed to leave. We all agreed that we would meet over Jay's when we were done. We gave our statements to the police. And them made sure Ayanna's parents were as ok as they could be under these circumstances.

What was turning out to be a wonderful day with my girls, turned so quickly into a nightmare. She was gone and there was nothing I could do about it.

Chapter Forty-Five

"Little Child Runnin' Wild"
— Curtis Mayfield

"Little Child Runnin' Wild"- Curtis Mayfield

Que-

I got the message from Mario. Jay and I were on our way to the spot. When we got there i noticed that there was a second car parked at the entrance. Jay and I looked at each other. We knew this was not a social call. We walked in ready to accept whatever the news was. MOre than likely it had to do with this shit that just went down.

I walked in and there with Mario was Sargent. Sargent was the Patriarch of the FAM.He never made an appearance unless some serious shit was about to hit the fan.

We sat down at the table and he poured us drinks.

There was long pause and then Sarg spoke.

"Que. Jay. The hit set off a string of shit that we can't get off our boots. The second nigga yall took out was an undercover NARC. He was sent in to try to get close to the Shaw Family. That bitch Toya was an informant. There is some serious heat coming our way. The block is hot, but the city is about to be on lockdown until they can catch whomever is connected to the shootin of that fuckin PIG." He took a sip of his brandy. He continue "This shit is about to do down, Yall family so we got to protect yall. We're sending you both away for a while. We got to keep everyone involved clean. We sent your soldiers south. WE are sending you two West. You'll be overseeing the operation in MIchigan until thing cool off here. You'll be compensated. We'll take care of everything. Mario will watch over the city for now. When everything cools off You'll be coming back and taking over for me. This shit really fucked things up boys, but it'll blow over." he said and finished his brandy.

We sat there. There wasn't much to say. We understood the lifestyle and we knew under the circumstances this was best. It was fucked up. This was really Fucked up.

I have one question " When do we leave" I asked.

"You have 2 days to wrap shit up here and be gone"

He handed us 2 duffel bags and instructions. And then walked out the door

We were fucked and there was nothing Jay and I could do. We had 2 days.

Fuck!!!!

Chapter Forty-Six

"Him Or Me"

– Today

"HIm or Me" -Today

Que

FUCK!!!

What am I doing. I know the lifestyle I live. I can't put her in this. I can't put her danger like this. I was trying to convince myself that Anika would be better off without me. THe truth of the matter was I would not be ok without her. I had a ring and I was planning on asking her to marry me. I had it all planned out. We was gonna do it up big. My baby deserved it. And now …. Fuck!!

She deserved better. Anika deserved more than I can give her. I could not ask this of her. I would not ask her. SHIT!!!

I knew what I had to do. As fucked up as this shit was, I loved Anika way too much for me not to do it.

I arrived at the JIm Kelly's Bar & Grill. It was located at the west end of the Man Place Mall. I wa early. I sat at the window table that was in the corner. I faced the door so that I could easily see what awaited me.

He walked in. We were polar opposites. But I could see what she saw in him. I guess if I was a clean cut mutherfucka, I would be like him. He must be a regular, cause a few of the bitches in there spoke up and greeted him by name. He saw me and headed in my direction. He sat down.

I had the waitress bring me a double shot of cognac. He ordered a rum and coke. This nigga.

There was silence. I spoke up.

"Thank you for meeting' I stated.

"You said it was about Anika so I came" He commented. " So is everything ok. Is she ok" he asked.

"Anika is as ok as she's going to be." I paused. " Do you know who I am" I asked

"Yeah, sort of" he replied.

"Then you know I love Anika. I love her with all I am. I been down for Ma since before you could catch a football. Do you love her. Do you love Anika? I demanded

" I do. I love her just like you. I would give my right hand , all my fame and glory to be with her. She is the first thing think of when I wake up and the last thing on my mind when I close my eyes at night" he confessed.

"What are your plans for her?, I mean do you love her enough to protect her and keep her safe?' I inquired.

"Yes. I want her to be my wife. I would never allow anything to happen to her. Why are you asking me these questions?" he asked.

"Because I love her. And I need to know that if I step aside, you will be the one to care for her, spoil her, protect her and love her. Give her what I can't. Can you do that?

Can you ?"

" Yes. I can do it. I'll take care of her.I promise" he spoke in a somber tone. He continued "Why are you stepping away. If you love her why not fight for her?"

"Because I would win. You don't have a leg to stand on when it comes to me and Anika's bond.

That girl has a hold on me that only god can break.I know her heartbeat, her thoughts and she knows mine. But i can't have what happen to Ayanna happen to her. I can't ask that of her. And because she will never leave me, I have to be the one to walk away. I love her that much to know that. So I'm moving out of your way. I need you to promise me on your life." I demanded.

"I will." he answered.

"Good because if you don't I will find you. If you hurt her, I will know, and if he break this promise I will kill you" I drank the rest of my cognac slamming the glass on the table breaking it as I walked out the bar.

Shit!!!!My heart

I thought grabbing my heart. I had never knew so much pain. Now I had to make my exit. 1 day left and I'm running out of time.

Chapter Forty-Seven

"Tell Me What You Want Me To Do"
— Tevin Campbell

"Tell Me What You Want Me to Do" -Tevin Campbell

Que

Without a doubt this is the hardest thing I have ever had to do. KIlling a nigga came easy compare to what I was about to do. When you kill a nigga it done. Butt breaking my promise to Anika, that shit will haunt me forever. I could not ask her to do this for me. It was the reason I resisted my feeling for her. It was the very reason I had walked away from her so many times. She doesn't belong in my world. Anika deserves better.I can't even accept that I have to tell her I need to leave.She will want to come with me. I just can't have her mixed up in this shit. NOPE! I can't fuckin do it! She is the only girl I ever loved, she's the only person i ever loved. And Dammit, It's the reason I have to let her go for now. She'll never forgive me. She'll hate me for her own good. I don't know if my heart will be ok with this, but for now it is what it is. Fuck it. I gotta go.

I walked out the door to the house. I left the package on the table. I knew she would see it. I just hope that one day she could forgive me. Because I was coming back for her hell or high water, I was going to make this shit right.

Anika

I had been sick to my stomach. At first I thought it was all of the stress I had been under. Then with what happen to Ayanna, I just can't take it. But I never imagined that this was the case. I don't even know what to do. I'm so torn and this makes things even harder. I waited so long for Que to tell me his feelings for me. But who knew I would have feelings for Mr. Cornerback. I know he cares for me too. It was so cute of him to to come to the hospital to be by my side. I am so torn. I wish my father had schooled me on what to do when you love women. There was no way I could chose, but now this makes everything that much harder. I'm pregnant. And one of these two fine men is the father of my child. ONe thing is for sure, I better make the right decision.

I arrived home but there was no sign of Que. I needed to lay down. Hopefully he will come home early tonight and we can talk. Some much has been going on. I just want to be honest with him. It was the only way we were going to be able to move forward in this relationship. Even if he was not the father of this baby I'm carrying. If he loved me we could make this work. We had too. IT was the only way.

I woke up and still no Que. I decided to cook dinner. Since I had been staying at Que's house, I mean our house. I had been making it my own. I brought groceries and little odds and ends that added that woman's touch. I finished dinner. I tried to wait for Que, but waiting for him I might starve. So I ate alone. I called Ayanna's parents to check on them.

They were busy planning the funeral. I told them I would help out with whatever they needed. I promised to stop by the house tomorrow. I also called Mr. cornerback and left a message on the answering machine. I knew he would return my call when he got in. He was busy with Preseason football stuff. HIs schedule was very rigorous right now. He told me that he would be busy during the week and that we would probably see each other during the week end. That was fine and dandy until Que confessed his love for me. Now I felt like I was avoiding him. I know I would need to end this, bt my heart… It sucks being in love .. IN love with two men.

It was getting late no call from Que or Mr. Cornerback. I could not wait up any longer. I would sleep and in the morning try these conversations all over again.

Jay

Yazz and I were all packed up. Once I told her, I could not convince her otherwise. She was coming and there was nothing I could say to stop her. In a way I was happy. She was my world. This would give me a chance to stack up and plan my exit game. I had mentioned it to Que in oking, but in all seriousness, the shit that had happened over this summer had me seriously thinking about getting out. I did not want to ever put Yazz in a situation that she would need to bury me over some bullshit. Nor would I want to ever put her back n the situation that endangered her life ever again. I think we just need to get out of the Low. Go somewhere and start over.

Que and I planned our exit. We had our orders. We would only be about 30 min away from each other. This way we kept our distance just incase someone was following us. Or tryna keep tabs. We had cash and were told everything else would be supplied. We would be running the West operation for the Fam until things cooled off in Buff. They wanted us to tighten up the shop and increase production and territory. It was the same ole same ole. But it was what we need and unfortunately we did that shit well. The only difference is this time I would have Yazz with me and by my side.

Yazz

I don't know why he even thought I was gonna stay my ass here while he leaves. And he couldn't tell me when he was coming back. Fuck that shit. He already knew. I was packed and ready to leave. tHe only thing was that I could not tell anyone. I could not say a word. I could call my family once we were gone and let them know I was ok. But I could not tell then where I was. It would compromise Jay and Que. As hard as it would be for me to leave Anika and Monica especially after what just happened to Ayanna, I had to go. I could not lose Jay too.I know they would be upset, but they would also understand. And if they were in my shoes they would do the same.

I keep telling myself that everything would be ok. I finished up some minor errands and finalized a few things. I was ready. We were leaving tonight. Just me and Jay. I would figure out what to tell my family later. I would call the girls once we got settled in. I knew someday we would be back, but for now it was goodbye Buffalo. Hello me and Jay.

Que

I got the music blasting in the car. Anything to take my mind off Anika. I almost turned around and went and got her. I can't believe this is the shitty as hand I've been dealt. I let her go and now I need to get her out of my mind. THat was harder said than done. I better slow down the speed limit is 65mph driving through Ohio. I just hit the turnpike. I guess the best thing about this is if that mutherfucka break his promise to me, I'll only be 7 hours away. I will be back in BUffalo before he can blink. I will not hesitate to murder his ass. I kept the foot on the pedal and let the sounds of Teddy Pendergrass cry my all the way to my designation. I will be back. I just hope she will forgive me.

Chapter
Forty-Eight

"When Will I See You Smile Again"
– Bell Biv Devoe

"When Will I See You Smile Again" Bell Biv Devoe

Anika

" Dear Anika ,

You're reading this letter, because I couldn't tell you face to face why I could not be there for you. Nothing would please me more Ma that to be there with you, holding you and loving you. BUt the lifestyle I lead doesn't always allow me to love without consequences.

It's fucked up I know. BUt I knew you would follow me and that's not what I want for you.

I love you and don't ever forget that. And it's because I love you, that I had to go and leave you behind.. I know you won't understand the things that are going down. BUt after what happen to Ayanna, I refuse to put you in any shit that might cause me to lose you. Ever.

I told you once before that everything I do is for you. And everything I said was the truth.I want you to stay in the house. I left you the bank account information. I had you name added so you don't have to want for anything. The keys to the car and most importantly you have my heart. I will be back for you. I just don't know when. It would be unfair of me to ask you to wait for me.So do you Ma. Don't worry I'll always have your back, no matter what happen while I'm gone. If you need anything let Mario know.

Remember Anika, I love you Ma. I'll make you smile again, promise. I'll be back for you when I can

Que"

A.A. LEWIS

Chapter Forty-Nine

"Can You Stand The Rain"
— New Edition

"Can You Stand The Rain"- New Edition

Monica

It was a beautiful service.I could barely make it upto the casket to say my good bye. I don't give a fuck what people say, that did not look on bit like Ayanna. NIggas swear if you throw some make up on a dead man's face, comb their hair and throw some nice close on them that they look like the person we have grown to know and love. Fuck that shit. She did not look like my sister. Even when me and Anika went up to the platform to sing. I could not look down at the casket. I had to just close my eyes and sang. Oh you didn't know Anika and I had mad voice skills.

We use to sing in the church choir and we went to Buffalo Academy for Visual and Performing Arts. We were PA Girls! In fact we all were, Yazz, Ayanna, me and Anika. So when I say we go back, we go back. our friendship, sisterhood was deep.

We sang "Take my hand Precious Lord". WE sang the shit out of that song. I don't think I've ever been brought to tears and felt the spirit over me like I did when I sang today. It was my final hello and goodbye to my sister. We brought down the church. With tears in my eyes, I sang my heart, my pain and love with every verse. It was my all i could give, my last plea to understand and to accept our being here. I think we did her proud. I thinks she was happy. I felt that she was at peace.

Anika

I never knew that Ayanna had touched so many people. The church was packed. It was standing room only. That was not hard to do at Mt. Ararat Baptist Church. The pastor gave a moving sermon. Many people got up to share their love for Ayanna. I think it gave her Parents the acknowledgement they needed.

Their words confirmed that they had raised a beautiful, bright and successful woman. They could be forever proud of that. Ayanna's mother asked MOnica and I to sing at the funeral. At first I declined. I did not know if I had the courage nor the strength to bare my soul in that way. I had too much going on and besides it had been a while since I stepped foot in a church. But I promised her that i would do whatever she needed me to do to help out. So I agreed.

When the announced me and Monica, we rose from the pew. Her Ayanna's mother had ask that we wear white to symbolize the innocence of Ayanna's life and to show we were part of her family. Monica was dressed in a white sleeveless silk knee length dress. It wrapped around her neck in a beautiful double bow. iT buttoned up the back.I wore a white linen silk A-Line dress.It had a white and black poka dot belt that cascaded in many layers down my right side. I wore a matching polka dot rose floral pin in my hair. As we walked by Ayanna's parents her mom touched our hands. WE smiled as she blow us a kiss. I touched the coffin.

Looking out at the congregation. My nerves took over. Monica just grabbed my. She squeezed and I closed my eyes and just belted out the first words of the song as practiced. BUt something happen. I allowed the song to speak through and to me. I sang. I sang like God was listening. lIke the angels were holding my up and lifting me to a higher plight. I sang for my dear sister, I sang for Yazz, I sang for que and Jay. BUt most importantly I sang for me. I sang for this unborn child I carried. I sang and tears fell. I sang and gave it to God. I gave him my pain and my heartache. I gave it to him. I sung so that he knew I was so sorry. THat I had forgotten that I could turn to him.THat I had neglected to speak to him. He had been my friend all along and I had turned my back and forgotten what a friend he is. And here I was asking him to take my sister and keep her in his love forever and ever and I had not been worthy to ask him for anything. I sang for his forgiveness. I sang and the most beautiful harmonies of love came pouring out. THe notes were perfect. The riffs were elegant. And monica and I left it all on the pulpit. There was nothing else we could give or ask. Ayanna was gone and we gave it to God. All the pain, love, joy and sorrow. He took it. He heard me and MOnica. And he gave us peace. He allowed me to breath, grieve and say good bye to my dear sister. I opened my eyes and still holding Monica's hand we walked of the platform and back to our seats.

Monica

Damn. I need a blunt after all this shit. I can't take it. I was standing outside the church. It was me Sam , Anika and Mr. Cornerback. Mario walked up to us and asked to speak to me and Anika. He handed us pagers. Said we should take them so that he could get a hold of us if he needed. He handed Anika an envelope. She placed it in her purse.

He was dressed in an all black suit. He looked real G. Sam and Mr. Cornerback were talking. I knew that Anika was hurting. Que was MIA and Yazz and Jay were gone. The timing was fucked up. I was going to have to make sure she was ok. We couldn't talk right now, but we would get up. Right now I needed a blunt. Losing Ayanna was one thing but with everyone gone, i felt like the family was breaking up. I couldn't handle this shit. It was too much.So I was out.

Anika

I waited with Ayanna's parents. I neede to make sure they were ok. Mr. cornerback was right there with me the whole time. He even kept Sam smiling which was hard to do under the circumstances. People were starting to leave. It had been a long day. Everyone commented on the song and monica s=and my singing. Mr. Cornerback teased and said he didn't know Monica and I could blow. I liked that it made him smile that I could surprise him from time to time. We said our goodbyes to Sam. I had his number so we would stay in touch.I liked Sam. He would have been perfect for Ayanna. They would have been. I could see them married with children, Just the thought makes me cry.

I turn to catch my composure and Mr.Cornerback pulls me into him. He holds me. He hands me his handkerchief. I cried and it was ok.

Mr. Cornerback opened the car door for me and helped me get in. He closed the door behind me and walked around to the driver side, got in and drove. He asked me where I would like to go. I told him to take me home. He looked puzzled. I told him to take me back to his house. Que had made his choice and it was time I made mine. If I could not have what I wanted I would have what I could. I was choosing Mr. Cornerback- Aaron. His name was Aaron. It was time I grew up. I had to stop chasing shit that was running after me. AAro had been good to me and could provide everything I needed and wanted. Most importantly I knew he loved me. He would now Love me and my unborn child. I would make his home my home and his world mines. When I said I left it all on the pulpit, I did.I left the pain, the tears and Que right there. He may come back, but I won't be waiting. Not anymore. I've waited enough and it was time I have a happy ending. It was time for me to start loving and living,

Chapter Fifty

"Return Of The Boom Bap"
- KRS-One

"Return of the Boom Bap"-KRS One

Aaron

It has been about 8 months since that NIgga Que up and left. He gave me the greatest gift a man could have, a family. Anika was pregnant and due in a month. She told me she wasn't sure if I was the father, but I did not care. I loved her so much. I told her no paternity test needed, if she was mine then so was the baby. I asked her to marry me and he said yes. Now I got the girl the baby and the career. That Punk Que don't scare me. That NIgga can never come between me and Anika now. Hell he ain't the only one with secrets. I just don't have to run away from mine.

Mario

I got a good hold on the city. Business is good and the FAM is happy. Que and Jay taught me well. In such a short time so much has changed. These streets are the same, it's just the bull shit that comes along with being in my position.

I got the all clear From Sargant. It was time for the changing of the guards. IT was time for my brothers to come home.

Jay

I'm alway impressed at what me and Que are able to do. MIchigan had become a major player for the FAM under our care. WE had groomed and cultivated the territory.

The only issue is what this move has done to Yazz. I knew she missed Anika and Monica. She didn't say it but I could see it in her eyes. BUt I had good news and I could not wait to share it.

Que

I got the call from Mario. I told Jay he could finish up things in Michigan. I was out. I had things to do and people to see. I was coming home BUffalo. I was coming back Anika.

www.ingramcontent.com/pod-product-compliance
Lightning Source LLC
Chambersburg PA
CBHW052015070526
44584CB00016B/1762